Anti-~Submarine Warfare

Anti-Submarine Warfare

Warfare Second edition

J.R. Hill

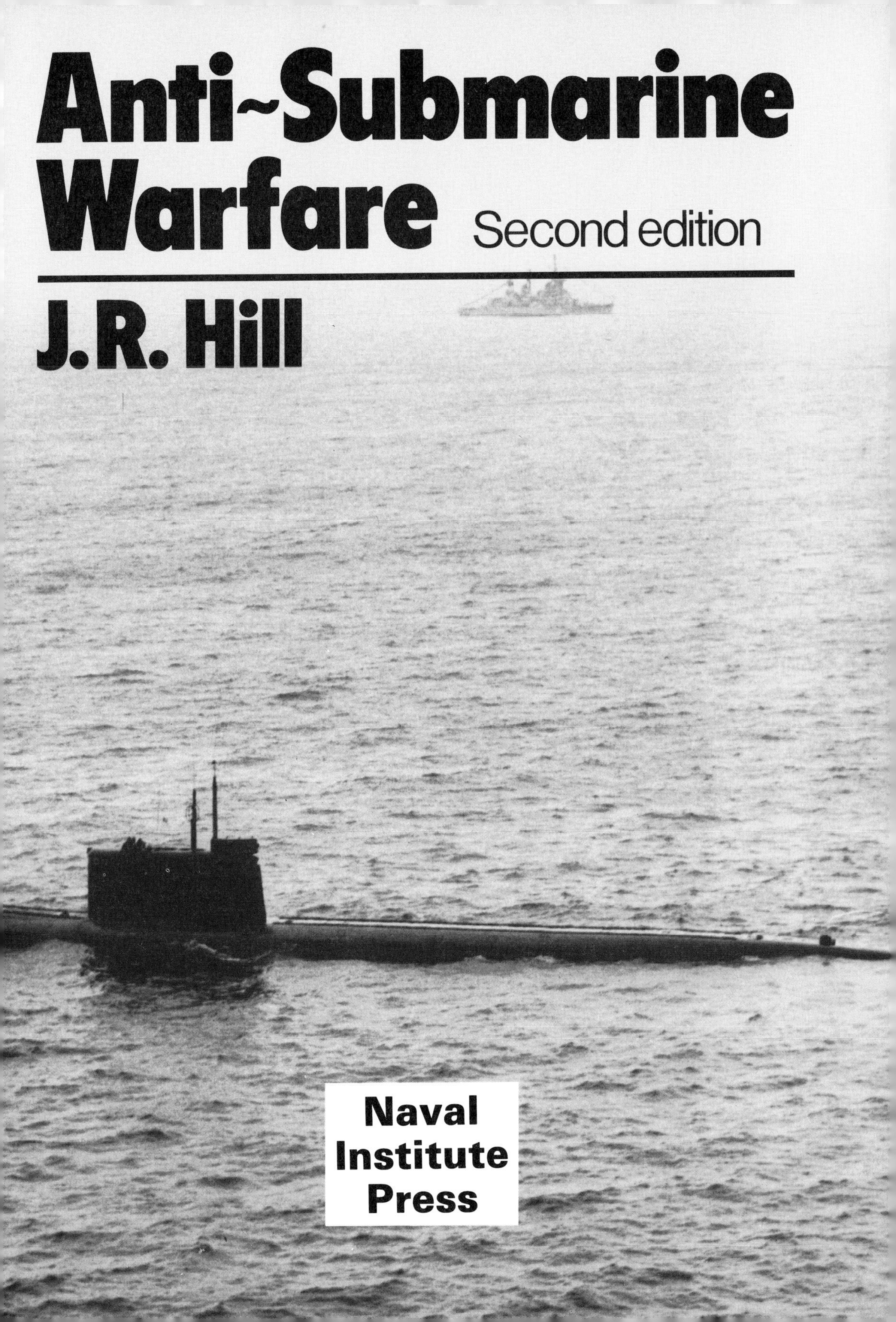

Naval
Institute
Press

First published 1984
US Edition 1985
US Second Edition 1989

The views expressed in this book are the author's own
and do not necessarily represent official opinion or
policy.

Published and distributed in the United
States of America by the Naval
Institute Press, Annapolis, Maryland 21402

Library of Congress Catalog Card No
89-60936

ISBN 0-87021-998-7

Manufactured in Great Britain

Contents

Previous page:
A Soviet 'Tango' Class submarine is shadowed by a Sea King of 820 Squadron FAA, attached to *HMS Invincible*, during 1984.
Crown Copyright

This page:
An RAF Nimrod stands by to receive its load of sonobuoys.
Dowty

Foreword

By Vice-Adm Sir Ian McGeoch KCB, DSO, DSC

Since this book was written, in 1983, there have been rapid and significant changes in three of the major factors with which the state of the art of anti-submarine warfare interacts, namely the international scene, US Naval strategy, and the technology of anti-submarine detection and its counter-measures. We have in the Soviet Union the era of *glasnost* and *perestroika*; in the United States the administration has wholeheartedly adopted what has been called 'President Reagan's Maritime Strategy'; and the Soviet Navy has succeeded in reducing the detectability of its newer submarines to levels comparable with those of the US Navy's own submarines and those of the Royal Navy.

It is a tribute to Adm Hill's authorship that these developments do not call for a revision of his text, other than in a few details, in order to maintain its authority; but I subscribe to the necessity, which he has accepted, of projecting 'Into the 1990s' a number of aspects of anti-submarine warfare which may be expected to change substantially in response to new factors. For example, strategic appreciations may no longer be based upon the assumption that one's own submarines enjoy a marked acoustic advantage over those of the potential enemy. Hence, unless it were to become practicable for one's own submarines to operate together as a tactical unit and thus to achieve a concentration of force against a hostile submarine, the outcome of a submarine versus submarine campaign must, in theory, be a draw.

As to the Maritime Strategy, it is in reality a politico-military concept founded upon the facts of geography, according to which any (grand) strategy adopted by the United States — other than complete isolationism within 'fortress America' — is bound to depend critically upon the ability of the United States and her allies to use the sea for their purposes while denying its use to any hostile coalition. Even so, it is possible to discern, in the North Atlantic region for example, the need continually to reconcile in practice the counter-vailing concepts of, on the one hand, the Maritime Strategy as an extension of the bounds of 'fortress America' to the shores of the Eurasian land-mass, as might be 'a moat defensive to a house, against the envy of less happier lands'; or, on the other, as the indispensable bridge to bring succour to friends and allies threatened by continental hegemonial ambitions and power.

It is currently fashionable to proclaim that 'just as on land NATO believes in forward defence, we have a strategy of forward defence at sea also'. Given the restoration of a comparable capacity for concealment to all the world's newer submarines, it might well be imprudent to act upon a direct analogy between defence of a land, and defence of a sea frontier. In the case of the former, penetration by hostile forces cannot remain for long undetected, and if unopposed would concede his aim to the aggressor; but in the latter case penetration (eg by submarine) may be virtually impossible to detect, let alone prevent, and would not of itself concede victory to the enemy. In war at sea the analogy with a forward defence on land is immediate defence — that is to say, to ensure that the enemy is at once brought to action with a superior force no matter how far forward (from his base) the targets which he attacks.

This new edition of *Anti-Submarine Warfare* provides much of the material needed upon which to base the most reliable net assessment of the balance between submarine warfare and its counter-measures likely to be accessible to the general public during the next decade.

Ian McGeoch

Castle Hedingham
14 January 1989

Acknowledgements

Being neither a submariner nor an anti-submarine specialist may have given me some advantages in writing this book; it has, for example, meant that there was no need to choke back a desire to deploy overmuch technical knowledge. On the other hand, to acquire the background that was necessary to interpret Anti-Submarine Warfare for the general reader, I needed to talk to a great many people on both sides of the Atlantic.

Among those who gave their time and knowledge to help me were Rear Adml Nigel Brodeur CF, Lt-Cdr John Bullock, Capt Don Cannell USN, Sqn Ldr Pat Carroll, Capt Chris Chamberlen, Dr Donald Daniel, Lt-Cdr Phil Dickinson, Capt Jan Einthoven RNethN, Cdr David Evans, Capt Hock USN, Capt Howard USN, Cdr Kennedy USN, Cdr Kirkland USN, Capt Mike Layard, Lt-Cdr Gerry McGeown, Prof Michael MacGwire, Mr K.J. Moore, Grp Capt Jim Morris, Lt Mike Nixon, Capt Parchem USN, Cdr Francis Ponsonby, Rear Adml Derek Reffell, Mr Geoffrey Rissone, Cdr Terry Smy, Rear Admiral Paul Speer USN, Cdre Spofford USN, Cdr Stoddart, Rear Adm Pat Symons, and Master Chief White USN. Others there are whose names are not recorded: I recall them with gratitude and hope they will forgive my failure to mention them specifically.

There was also a great need for photographs to illustrate this rather unphotogenic subject, and here I was helped not only by some of those mentioned above but by many organisations and individuals beside. They included, from British industry, Mr Freddie Crewe, Mr Giles Harvey, Mr Peter Lindley and Miss Joanna Losack; from Service organisations, Lt-Cdr Coombes, FCPO Dargan, CPO Drew, Mr Link, CPO Smart and Mr Speakman. Historical material was provided by two people to whom I am particularly grateful, Lt-Cdr Robbie Robinson of HMS *Vernon* and Mr Willis of the Imperial War Museum. Thanks also to my Nimrod pilot, Flt Lt Martin Christy, and to Bob Downey who produced the line drawings.

Finally, very special thanks are due to certain people who were prime movers in critical areas of my research. These were: Vice Adm Sir John Cox for some hours' fascinating discussion and a visit to the Royal Naval Air Station, Culdrose; AVM George Chesworth for the same, and a visit to Royal Air Force Kinloss and a flight in a Nimrod; Vice Adm Sir David Hallifax, Capt Jeremy Read and Lt Peter Gilbert for their splendid organisation of my visit to the United States; Mr Lawrence Phillips for an excellent day at sea with the Fleet; Lt-Cdr Vic Hardcastle for an introduction to all the official books that I could properly see; Capt Ian Sutherland for the sort of help that authors hope for from a Director of Public Relations (Navy); and Simon Forty and the rest of the team at Ian Allan Ltd. Without them, there would have been no book.

Below:
Shipborne anti-submarine assets can include fixed-wing aircraft if the carrier is of sufficient size.
Official US Navy photograph

Introduction

Concealment is often a sign of guilt. It is not surprising, therefore, that the evolution of the submarine called forth more moral indignation than any previous weapon of war. The most famous quotation from those early years around the turn of the century is probably Admiral Sir Arthur Wilson's:

'. . . underhand . . . and damned un-English . . . treat all submarines as pirates in wartime . . . and hang all the crews.'

But he was echoed in many another country, and not only by traditionalist naval officers like himself. The rather clean and manly image of sea-fighting was blurred by these craft that were able to hide, then strike, then hide again.

Moreover, what was to be done about them? Initially many naval thinkers were complacent; the craft were small, unreliable and of poor endurance under water and seakeeping above water. The more imaginative, however, saw that these difficulties could be overcome to make the submarine a potent weapon system, against which no countermeasures currently existed. They might have judged that the search for means of combatting submarines would be unending, complex and very expensive. They would have been right.

As will be apparent throughout this book, successful anti-submarine warfare demanded two widely different though interactive skills: the technical and the tactical. The tactical side of ASW depends not only on the technology available to both sides, but on what the submarines are trying to do and how they are trying to do it. It was in this matter that the greatest early miscalculations were made.

Probably it was natural that forces brought up on the doctrines of Alfred Mahan, as both British and German navies were before World War 1, would expect the prime use of submarines to be in fleet action. After all, Mahan had laid down that command of the sea was the essence of sea power and, in war, was to be achieved by the possession of a dominant battle fleet; dominance could be achieved either by having a fleet so powerful that the opponent was unable to offer battle, or by victory in fleet action against an opponent who did offer it.

Of course World War 1 turned out quite differently. It proved very difficult to integrate submarines into fleet action; their navigation, sensors and communications were all too unreliable; put succinctly, they didn't know and you couldn't tell them. What submarines did turn out to be good at was a form of warfare that Mahan had tended to dismiss as inherently indecisive: the *guerre de course* against trade shipping. In fact, they were so good at it that, given the vulnerability of the Allies and particularly Britain to pressures on their ocean-going trade, the unrestricted campaign against merchant shipping in 1916 very nearly settled the war in Germany's favour. Two things

8

Bottom left:
The new menace: submarines passing HMS
***Dreadnought* in the early years of the 20th century.**
National Maritime Museum

Above:
**Contrary to many expectations the main
effectiveness of submarines in World War 1 was
against commerce, and their most usual form of
attack was gunfire.**
Imperial War Museum

Below:
**An airship over a convoy in World War 1. The
institution of convoy in 1917 turned the tide against
the U-boats, and air cover for convoys dramatically
increased their effectiveness still further.**
Imperial War Museum

stopped that happening: first, the institution of the campaign itself was decisive in bringing the United States into the war; second, the Allies' adoption of the convoy system in 1917 reduced the number of targets available for U-boats, focused their activities into areas where war ships (and often aircraft) were present, and thereby vastly increased their problems while diminishing our own. The balance swung, the lifeline was preserved.

Neither of these developments was technical. However, some advances in anti-submarine technology had been made. The earliest efforts, around 1905, came to very little; they included towed charges and grapnels, an indicator net that dipped a flag when a submarine was caught in it, and a lassoo for catching submarines. Pehaps it is not too unkind to think that hunting, shooting and fishing had had some effect on the inventive imagination of the Navy at that time. But by 1914 wire explosive sweeps had been developed which would give some chance of sinking an unwary submarine (and alarming a wary one) in the shallow waters of the North Sea and Channel, the areas where fleet action was expected. Primitive depth charges were soon available, too.

But a much more fundamental development was taking place on both sides of the Atlantic: everyone began to realise that underwater sound was the key to detecting a submerged submarine. Fixed hydrophone stations began to be established in 1915; by the end of 1917 there were 21 around the coast of the United Kingdom. This was all very well

Above:
An early anti-submarine weapon, the Lance Bomb.
Imperial War Museum

Left:
The first anti-submarine mortar, mounted in a converted trawler, 1916. *Imperial War Museum*

for coastal defence, but as we have seen the main threat was elsewhere; and, after the formation of the Anti-Submarine Division at the Admiralty in December 1916, hydrophones went to sea in ships in increasing numbers. The Nash Fish, a towed hydrophone that could even indicate the direction of a noise source, was first fitted in July 1917. For visual detection, aircraft patrols were increasingly useful, particularly as U-boats had to spend much time on the surface for battery charging.

The development of echo-ranging as a detection system – then called Asdics, now termed active sonar, and described more fully in Chapter 3 – was too late to affect the course of World War 1. The first Asdic set was fitted in a destroyer in 1920. But thereafter fitting continued rapidly, and so did the training of operators. After initial doubts, with a particularly critical period in the late 1920s, the British fleet acquired great confidence in its ability

to detect and sink submerged submarines. In a limited way, this was put to the test during the Spanish Civil War. German and Italian submarines had been preying on the shipping supplying the Republican forces, and by the Nyon Arrangement British warships were empowered to depth charge submarine contacts which displayed hostile intent. Some cautionary tales came out of the 'Nyon Patrol'; the most telling of them begins the Epilogue to this book. Perhaps they were not heeded quite enough.

For at the start of World War 2, although some things were got right – the most important being the immediate adoption of convoy for merchant shipping – others were quite severely miscalculated.

Above left:
The hydrophone was recognised as a critically important detection device early in World War 1. A rudimentary towed array in the Otranto Barrage, 1918. *Imperial War Museum*

Left:
Desperate measures for desperate times: an anti-submarine gun concealed in a trawler deckhouse during World War 1. *Imperial War Museum*

Below:
A tell-tale oil and air bubble after an attack: in spite of the crudity of much of the weaponry, 180 U-boats were sunk during World War 1.
Imperial War Museum

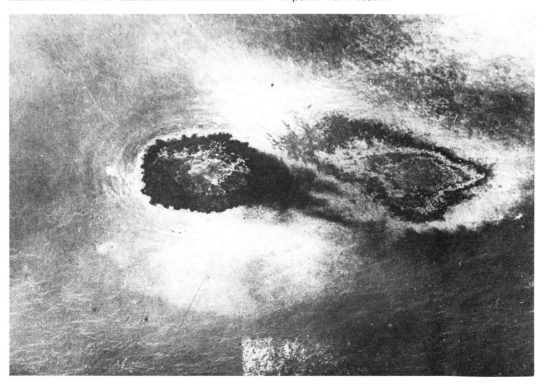

There were far too few small anti-submarine escorts; convoy tactics had not been sufficiently exercised; the potential of shore-based aircraft was woefully under-used. Moreover, the Royal Navy was surprised by the tactics of the U-boats. True enough, what they were trying to do – mainly to sink merchant ships – had been correctly predicted; but how they were going about it had not. They were spending far more time on the surface than had been expected, using their speed in the surfaced mode to close in on, and keep up with, the slowly-moving convoys. With their low profiles they were very difficult to see, particularly at night. If menaced, they could of course submerge; and once they did, the Asdic proved a much less reliable detection system than had been expected, and the depth charge a less certain means of destruction.

Thus, the technical improvements during World War 2 occurred in a much wider field than might have been expected. They included centimetric radar for both escorts and aircraft to detect surface submarines; high-frequency direction-finding to pinpoint submarines communicating with others in the same 'wolf-pack'; longer-range aircraft fitted with Leigh Lights for night attack; small aircraft carriers to operate with convoys; decryption of Doenitz's command messages to submarines at sea. Allied to the more obvious improvements to ships' Asdics and the associated weaponry, these turned the technical scale.

But they were greatly helped by tactical developments. Much greater skill in the handling and routeing of convoys steadily increased the U-boats' need to manoeuvre and expose themselves. The co-ordination of Operational Intelligence from

Right:
The immediate institution of convoy in World War 2 was a correct decision in spite of a shortage of escort vessels and aircraft. *HMS Vernon archives*

Below:
While neither as accurate nor as lethal as expected, the depth charge was still the main submarine killing weapon of World War 2. *HMS Vernon archives*

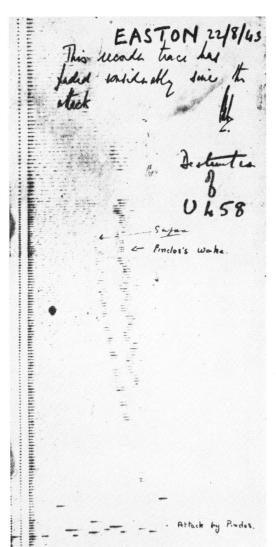

EASTON 22/8/43

This records trace has faded considerably since the attack

Destruction of

U 458

Sepa.

← Pinclos's wake.

Attack by Pindos.

all sources, and its dissemination to all who needed to know, reduced the opposition's ability to exploit surprise. Escorts' reaction to sinkings within the convoy, or indications of submarines' presence on its peripheries, became less haphazard, more and more based on mathematical principles and knowledge of the enemy's capabilities and tactics. The integration of aircraft into convoy support operations was immensely valuable in keeping down the wary submarine and destroying the foolhardy one. Finally, the institution of support groups, which operated some distance from a convoy and moved in against the submarines which were concentrating on it, was a notable tactical success.

Towards the end of the war the resources available to the Anti-submarine forces were truly formidable. By August 1943 over 2,600 vessels of the RN alone were Asdic-fitted; nearly 1,000 were major warships and as many aircraft were employed on ASW duties. They combined to make life intolerably difficult for the U-boats, even those that had been modernised. In some cases the well-named operation 'Swamp' did indeed fulfil the anti-submariner's dream of sanitising a relatively large area of sea.

Nevertheless, as the decade after the war's end brought a newly perceived threat from the Soviet Union, no one in the anti-submarine world was over-sanguine about the prospect of coping with it.

Left:
The visual accompaniment to Asdic's constant pinging in the ears: a range recorder trace.
HMS Vernon archives

Below:
Submarines were often literally blown to the surface: U70, sunk by HMS *Wolverine* on 7 March 1941.
HMS Vernon archives

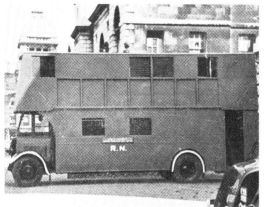

Above:
Operator training was all-important and took place ashore as well as afloat – sometimes in odd-looking locations. *(Top):* **The interior of the bus (upper deck).** *HMS Vernon archives*

Right:
Even the earliest nuclear-powered submarines looked like what they were: a new and formidable threat to other sea users. *NATO photograph*

Part of the reason for this lay in submarine developments which the Germans had only just failed to bring into general service by the end of the war and whose technology quickly became available to both East and West. Boats powered by the conventional system of diesels on the surface and battery-operated motors underwater received a great boost to their efficiency by the schnorkel or snort mast, which enabled them to run on diesels and thereby recharge batteries while at periscope depth. This, combined with batteries of greater capacity and improved acoustic sensing devices, made them much more effective *underwater* platforms.

But lurking in the minds of the scientists and engineers was something much more fundamental: the application of nuclear power to submarine propulsion. The first programme was set in hand in the USA in 1948, and the writer recalls the problems it raised being spoken of in the Anti-Submarine School in early 1949. It is right to say that it was viewed then with the greatest apprehension. No one was quite sure how to cope with an opponent whose underwater endurance was virtually unlimited and whose underwater speed might match the fastest surface ship.

With the advent of the true submarine the focal plane of anti-submarine operations, which had been close to the interface between sea and sky, began to sink into the depths. One factor which might have been expected to keep it close to the surface – the need to maintain a supply of fresh air for the submarine's crew – was overcome by technology, to be precise by the invention of the carbon dioxide scrubber. Two others were more difficult to the submariners to defeat completely. It was still sometimes necessary, if operating tactically against surface ships, to come shallow to gain intelligence of the full situation; and there was a maximum depth at which wireless aerials could pick up signals from the shore command or co-operating forces. But both these constraints were operational rather than physical and could be minimised by the individual submarine commander, so long as the organisation of the submarine force allowed him enough flexibility to do so.

Particularly as the technical problems surrounding nuclear-powered submarines were solved by the major maritime powers at a very rapid rate, a new or modified set of roles for the submarine could be considered. Since, as we have seen, what the submarine is trying to do greatly affects the measures adoped against it, it is worth stating these roles in this Introduction. Some were first thought of by the Americans, some by the Russians; that does not greatly matter, though the priority now given to them does, and will form part of the discussion later in the book.

Strategic Deterrence

Involving the ability to strike with nuclear weapons at an enemy's vital functions, strategic deterrence is an entirely new role for submarines, and is very closely linked with nulear propulsion, although early strategic missiles were carried in conventionally-powered boats and it is just possible to envisage that happening again. The classical mode, however, adopted by the USA, USSR, UK, France and probably China, is a large nuclear-powered hull carrying upwards of a dozen long-range ballistic nuclear-headed missiles which can be launched from a submerged position. The submarine's design and mode of operation can be optimised to avoid detection; that is to say, it can be made quite quiet, with excellent sensors, and operated at slow speeds and the most favourable depths. It does need a turn of speed to escape a detecting unit if it is located, and self-defence weapons for use if it comes under attack in war; but generally its job is to avoid trouble and preserve its potential to deter war. As we shall see, a Soviet writer would not put it in those terms because Soviet philosophy is somewhat different, but they will do as a general statement at this stage.

Tactical Employment against Surface Combatants

This may be linked with land operations (for example, it could be conducted against opposing amphibious forces) or may be a function or generalised sea warfare. It is probably the other end of the scale from stragetic deterrence, so far as submarine operations are concerned. If the ballistic missile submarine is bent on avoiding trouble, the submarine employed against an opposing fleet has to be looking for it. It can be sure that a variety of aircraft and warships will be doing their best to detect it; high value targets will be using a lot of speed; all units will manoeuvre to create the maximum sonic confusion, and to occupy the best water for sonar effectiveness. To get close enough for an effective torpedo attack on heavy unit may be extremely difficult even for a nuclear-powered boat. The stand-off possibilities of submarine-launched terminally-guided missiles can be exploited, though

for the shorter-range ones the boat may have to operate in a manner that risks detection while the fire-control solution is worked out, and the longer-range ones demand a forward-based sensor, which may itself be vulnerable, to indicate the target.

Tactical Employment against Shipping
This, the classical role of U-boats in two world wars (and incidentally of British submarines in the Mediterranean, and American submarines in the Pacific, in World War 2) has probably changed not so much in style as in scale. We shall discuss in Chapter 5 the vexed question of whether to convoy or not to convoy but whatever measures are adopted by the defence, the attacker is more likely to use torpedoes than anything else, and will come to close quarters in order to do so. Given the very large amount of shipping that needs to be defended, there will always be a shortage of defending forces and that will mean that both nuclear and conventionally powered submarines have a fighting chance against them. More than any other form of

submarine warfare, an anti-shipping campaign is an attrition struggle, lending itself to quite precise calculation of exchange rates: a cold, profit-and-loss business.

Tactical Employment against other Submarines
It is always a toss-up whether to class submarines which are used in the anti-submarine role as submarines or as anti-submarine forces. But here I do the former for, I think, good reasons. Once a submarine goes hunting for another it is, in effect, like fighting like; and, moreover, down there in the depths there may be more than one on either side. The first shot tends to go to the fellow who hears most, first; this may or may not be the hunter. But even if it is, the hunted may have a friend who can take swift revenge. Of all the employments of submarines now expected, this is the most untried; there has never been a submarine-versus-submarine action in war with both boats fully submerged at all points.

Inshore Operations
Submarines, almost certainly of the conventional sort only, can be employed on a variety of operations close to enemy shores: surveillance, minelaying, landing raiding parties, deploying midget craft, interfering with civil and military installations on the seabed and at shore terminals.

Above:
Strategic deterrence was an entirely new role for submarines, made possible by compact ballistic missiles and nuclear power: HMS *Repulse* in 1971. *Crown Copyright*

There will not be much room in this book to discuss all these points of the inshore war, but it must be said here that a country with a long coastline may be hard put to it to provide forces in sufficient numbers to dissuade a determined opponent from such attacks.

So, then, this book will discuss how the current anti-submarine art seeks to counter submarines carrying out all the functions described above. It will do so predominantly in the NATO context, for that is the most complex and therefore the most complete case. But it will take more than a passing look at Soviet anti-submarine philosophy, for surely that must itself have some effect on how the NATO case turns out. It will also touch, from time to time, on the submarine capabilities of countries around the world that belong neither to NATO nor to the Warsaw Pact, and mention some ASW problems associated with them. The Falklands campaign is too fresh in the memory for such factors to be ignored.

However, that campaign does raise a general point about submarine and anti-submarine warfare that needs making in this chapter and is perhaps a suitable one with which to end it. As was shown by the public impact of submarine operations in the Falklands, particularly the sinking of the *General Belgrano*, once a submarine fires its weapons it is in

a war situation and not one of uneasy or even violent peace, or tension, or low-intensity operations or any of the other phrases we have come to use to describe the half-world between normal international relations and armed conflict. The first use of the submarine weapon will always, therefore, be an important step in escalation, to be decided by government, and so probably will be any decision to prosecute submarine contacts to destruction. Anti-submarine readiness and preparations may precede such a decision, indeed they ought to do so in order that escalation by the other side may be deterred; but once anti-submarine warfare begins in earnest, the rules of engagement within the area of conflict may be expected to be fairly liberal. That will be a basic assumption of this book, although special considerations – notably about nuclear weapons – will be mentioned where they are appropriate. Anti-submarine warfare, then, is warfare indeed, the dominating factor in many naval operations and maritime defence budgets. Things have developed pretty fast since 1900.

The Threat

A discussion of the Soviet submarine force might logically begin with Soviet requirements as seen by them, go on to trace their submarine development in the light of those requirements, state their likely concepts of operations and deployments, and predict future developments that would improve their capacity to meet their needs. That would be it, pure and simple.

As Oscar Wilde observed, truth is never pure and rarely simple; and the evolution of the Soviet submarine force has certainly not been as smooth or as rational as the sequence above would imply. Moreover, no Soviet authority has told anything like the full story where Western ears can hear it; so any assessment has to be a matter of putting together all the published evidence (material and verbal) that is available, and trying from that to arrive at a reasonably coherent account of the why and the how, as well as the mistakes and mistimings, of the Soviet submarine effort.

First, it is necessary to try and establish what the overall Soviet aims are, for if they are not adversary to the West, if they would in no conceivable circumstances fight us, then there is no threat and I ought to be writing this chapter about Argentina. The evidence is otherwise. Right the way through Marxism-Leninism runs the supposition that the advance of Communism, in the face of hostile bourgeois-capitalist forces, is an inevitable historical process; but it is incumbent on every Communist to further that process by all the means in his or her power, and essential at the same time to preserve the movement's power-base in Soviet Russia. We thus get a constant, dynamic pressure outwards from a heavily-guarded centre. Alarmists in the West emphasise the pressure, pointing out quite rightly that if allowed to prevail it would impose what we would experience as an intolerable, alien tyranny. The counter-alarmists over-emphasise the guarding of the centre, suggesting that the Russians are too preoccupied with protection against what they see as encircling hordes to have any spare effort for furthering Communism. In my view, both errors of emphasis

are dangerous. If translated into policies, they could induce serious instability in the international system by making the Soviet Union on the one hand desperate, or on the other over-confident. It follows that a middle-of-the-road policy for the West is best; and if that looks rather like George Kennan's 'Containment' strategy of the early 1950s, well, that strategy always looked pretty sound and respectable to me.

That paragraph was no digression, for the adversary relationship, the Soviet dynamic and the Russians' preoccupation with the preservation of their territory and system are all essential ingredients of Soviet strategy and therefore of the premises on which their submarine force is founded.

For a start, it is clear that the Soviets regard any large scale war against the West as a final, ultimately nuclear, clash between two fundamentally opposed enemies that will end in extinction for one and victory for the other. One consequence of this view is that the Soviets are cautious about steps that might lead to war. They believe that it would cause very great damage to them, whatever the outcome. The other major consequence, however, is that they do their best to ensure that if war does occur, they are prepared to fight and win it. That their capacity to do this may deter the West from embarking on warlike courses is, it seems, not central to their theory; it is the war-fighting and war-winning ability that matters. (Indeed, this is a point Western disarmers miss when they react with horror if their own governments even toy with the idea of nuclear-war-fighting, while by some double standard they seem to think it all right for the Russians to have an out-and-out nuclear war-fighting philosophy). War-fighting does not necessarily mean using nuclear weapons straight away, it simply means using them when the military need is seen. It also means controlled use; the Russians do not envisage spasm warfare, and certainly put great stress on the retention of enough nuclear capacity, at the end of any exchange, to influence the final outcome decisively.

In general terms, this view of warfare can be

derived from Soviet writing, in particular the 'Military Strategy' of Sokolovsky. So far as the sea element is concerned, the chief authority is 'The Sea Power of the State', under the name of none other than Fleet Admiral Gorshkov, Commander-in-Chief of the Soviet Navy for over a quarter of a century and clearly its principal architect. Like much Russian writing in translation, it is often obscure in its language, which in any case is overlaid by Marxist polemic that may or may not be the Admiral's.

Nevertheless many strands of argument stand out clearly. One of the clearest is Gorshkov's distinction between 'Fleet against Fleet' and 'Fleet against Shore' – and the evident priority he gives to the latter. What he means by 'Fleet against Shore' is not primarily the projection of power in remote places by the Naval Infantry, but the strategic use of massive nuclear force from the sea against the vitals of the opponent. So much is clear from the context. If Gorshkov gives priority to seaborne strategic nuclear forces, so should we in this discussion.

Strategic Submarine Forces

Some commentators suggest that the very first Soviet attempts at deploying nuclear assets against the shore from submarines were in the early 1950s in the form of nuclear-headed torpedoes to be fired into harbours, and crude cruise missiles of a few hundred miles' range. I know of no evidence to suggest that these weapons, which certainly existed, were strategic in intent, but the Navy may of course have presented them as such in Soviet military counsels to show its interest in the strategic role.

For the weapons of undoubted strategic intent were already under development. In 1955 the first SS-N-4 ballistic missile was tested, and within two years this 300-mile range megaton-warhead, liquid-fuelled weapon was at sea in a conventionally-powered, specially converted 'Z' class submarine. In 1958 the specially designed 'Golf' class began to enter service. These too were conventionally-powered; they carried only three missiles and had to surface in order to fire them. Compared with Polaris, which went to sea only four years later, the system had many deficiencies. The limitations on range and submerged endurance meant that a 'Golf' class must expose itself often in US-dominated waters if it wished to remain within striking distance of its targets. In fact, they never did set up a regular patrol pattern. It was a 'Golf' class that was lost in the Pacific in 1968 (the salvage attempt by the Americans in the *Glomar Explorer* in 1974 is no doubt an epic, but one never perhaps to be told fully) and, in general, the Russians must have felt that the class was a first attempt from which many lessons, both technical and in terms of force requirements, could be learnt. Nevertheless 13 of the class, with longer-range missiles, are still in service, split between the Baltic and Pacific in the theatre role: an example of the way Russian naval forces, no less than any others, can change roles in the course of their lives.

All subsequent strategic missile boats were to be nuclear-propelled. First came the 'Hotel' class, which still mounted only three missiles and at first had to surface in order to fire them. However, a modification that entered service about 1964 gave them longer-range (750 nautical miles) missiles that could be fired from under water. All these

Below:
A Soviet ballistic missile submarine of the 'Golf' class. Missiles are housed in the fin.
Crown Copyright

19

developments, particularly nuclear propulsion,
were a long step towards a viable strategic seaborne
weapon system, but there were still many problems
from a Soviet point of view. The boats were noisy,
the first-generation powerplant not very reliable,
and the range of the missiles entailed a very long
transit to patrol areas that were uncomfortably close
to the USA and far from the home bases in
Polyarnoe (Kola Peninsula) and Petropavlovsk
(Kamchatka).

These problems were not solved by the next
generation of ballistic missile submarines, the
'Yankee' class, which appeared in large numbers –
peaking at 34 – between 1967 and 1974. True, they
had many more missiles; 16 were carried, in a

compartment abaft the fin which was much closer to
the configuration that had been made classical by
the American, British and French designs. But the
1,500-mile range of the missiles still meant that
ocean patrols were necessary and that even then
some parts of the United States could not be
threatened. There are many indications, moreover,
that in the face of improving US sonic systems the
boats' noise still exposed them to detection. So
although standing patrols were set up in the Atlantic
and Pacific, they were not so numerous as might
have been expected from an analysis of number and
serviceability. Some commentators regard this as a
reflection of Soviet strategic thinking and their
insistence on keeping forces in reserve; that may be
part of the reason, but their unwillingness to trust
any but the most reliable commanding officers and
crews, and their unease at exposing a high
proportion of their strategic forces far from home
areas, must be a contributory cause. The 'Yankees'
are still in service, though eight have had their

missile tubes removed in response to the requirements of the SALT-II treaty, the provisions of which both sides have agreed to honour in spite of its non-ratification by the United States Senate.

The next generation of Soviet ballistic missile submarines came much closer to their objective of a securely deployable strategic force. This was the 'Delta' class, delivered in the second half of the 1970s and deploying missiles of sufficient range to reach targets in the continental United States from patrol stations in the Barents and Okhotsk Seas. These seas are adjacent to the Soviet Union and, by the use of the maritime forces at their disposal, the Soviets can make them difficult for access for any opposing forces seeking to threaten their ballistic missile submarines. Gorshkov constantly stresses the desirability of using maritime forces in this way to protect the main striking force. The large missiles are too long to be accommodated flush with the submarine's upper deck and so the boat's silhouette is singularly humpbacked where the missile tubes penetrate the casing. Whether this gave operational disadvantages or not, the Russians built upwards of 30 'Deltas' in their great yards at Severodvinsk in the White Sea and Komsomol'sk on the Amur River.

It appears, however, that the Russians were not satisfied with the 'Delta' as a final solution. From the late 1970s there was talk of the 'Typhoon' weapon system and in 1980 the first of these monstrous vessels was launched. The concept appears to be, quite simply, a submarine battleship. It is said to have a displacement of 30,000 tons dived and to carry 20 missiles of a new type, almost certainly with multiple independently-targetted re-entry vehicles (MIRVs) as warheads. Speed is uncertain, but there is no reason for a very large vessel to be a slow one, indeed a greater wetted surface theoretically means a greater speed potential. But the most daunting statistic is its 75ft beam, which could mean a well-separated double hull with all the advantages of protection that that implies: in effect, rather like the 'torpedo bulges' that battleships used to have. If, in addition, the hulls are of titanium alloy as some reports suggest, it could be a very hard nut to crack. So now, in

Table 1: Soviet Ballistic Missile Submarines

| | | | Submarines | | | | | | Missiles | |
Number in service	Class	Entered service	Propulsion	Displacement submerged (tons)	Length (ft)	Beam (ft)	Type	Range (nm)	Launch mode	Number per boat
15*	Golf	1958-62	Diesel-electric	3,000	321	28	SS-N-5	750	Surfaced	3
6*	Hotel	1958-62	Nuclear	5,500	377	30	SS-N-5	750	Submerged	3
25*	Yankee	1967-74	Nuclear	9,300	425	38	SS-N-6	1,620	Submerged	16
18	Delta I	1973-77	Nuclear	10,000	446	38	SS-N-8	4,200	Submerged	12
4	Delta II	1975-76	Nuclear	11,000	500	39	SS-N-8	4,200	Submerged	16
14	Delta III	1976-82	Nuclear	11,000	492	39	SS-N-18	4,000	Submerged	16
2+	Typhoon	1981-	Nuclear	30,000	600	75	SS-N-20	4,500	Submerged	20

*Includes trials and training for advanced missiles   (This and subsequent tables are correct to 1984)

addition to the advantages of operation from their own semi-enclosed seas – 'defended ocean bastions', as one commentator puts it – the Russians are attempting to make their ballistic missile submarines physically invulnerable as well.

Of course one must be careful not to make the Russians ten feet tall (though it looks as if the 'Typhoon' is the one sort of submarine that could accommodate a ten-foot-tall Russian). They may simply have become obsessed with physical size, or felt they had to match and surpass the big American 'Ohio' class, or have been constrained by missile dimensions. And the 'Typhoon' may have operational and logistic disadvantages of which we know nothing. Nevertheless it is undeniably an impressive achievement, it would require great expenditure of resources to neutralise it, and it raises the question whether, mutual deterrence being a desirable state of affairs, any serious attempt need be made to do so. Indeed that queston has been apparent at least since the introduction of the 'Delta' class. An attempt to answer it will be made in Chapter 5.

In 1984 it was reported that the Soviet Union had developed a submarine-launched cruise missile, with a range of 1,900 nautical miles, for use against land targets. It could be fired from a submarine's torpedo tubes.

Submarine Forces for Use against Surface Ships

It would have been comfortable to divide this section into the same categories as Chapter 1 indicated, that is to say submarines for use against surface combatants and submarines for use against trade shipping. But, particularly in the case of Soviet submarines, it would be misleading to do that, for so many classes of submarine could be employed in either role; and in most cases it is by no means certain which role they were designed for, let alone whether there has been a role-change since.

In World War 2 Soviet submarines engaged both merchant and war vessels as opportunity offered, and there is not much indication of an overall concept of operations or any objective other than inflicting damage on the enemy. In statistical terms it was not particularly effective, due partly to the relatively low intensity of sea operations compared with the massive scale of the war on land, and partly to the inexperience of the submarine crews.

In the decade after 1945, the Soviets under Stalin embarked on a very large submarine building programme, envisaging well over 500 conventionally powered and armed boats. It is now the received wisdom that this was to support the defence of the Soviet Union against amphibious forces and only incidentally to interdict ocean-going shipping. If we had access to the records of all Soviet counsels over those years, that might turn out to be an incomplete answer. My guess is that the potential flexibility of a large submarine force, a high proportion of which was ocean-going, was in the back of a good many minds even if one of them was not Stalin's – which of course would have been quite enough to keep the prudent quiet.

At any event, at the beginning of the Gorshkov era – which coincided effectively with the rise of Khrushchev to power – the building of the 'Whiskey' and 'Zulu' classes was in full swing. Both designs owed a good deal to the German technology acquired in 1945. The 'Whiskey' was a medium-range boat of just over 1,000 tons, snort-fitted and totally conventional in its diesel and electric motor propulsion and its torpedo armament, with the exception that Soviet practice appeared to allow the widespread deployment of torpedoes with nuclear warheads. Over the years 'Whiskey' class submarines have been used as test-beds for a variety of new weapon systems and many have been transferred to foreign navies: all evidence of a solid, reliable design.

The 'Zulu' was a larger submarine, with a long cruising range and probably a slightly higher

underwater speed than the 'Whiskey'. It had the distinction of being the first submarine to be adapted for ballistic missile launch; six were so modified. But it was basically an unsophisticated boat, and like the 'Whiskey' showed little sign of any quietening measures. At this stage, clearly, the Russians were still emphasising quantity rather than quality; and the evidence suggests that in the early to middle 1950s they were thinking of very large quantities indeed of 'Whiskeys', 'Zulus' and their evolutionary successors.

But with the death of Stalin, change was in the air. At first it may almost have been change for the sake of change; there was much experiment and casting about, and it was not until the late 1950s that a coherent drive was made to reformulate military and naval objectives and concepts. But it is clear that two new factors now concerned the Russians. The centre of their system would soon be threatened from the sea by Polaris missiles; and many important operational targets, maybe even the vitals themselves, were already under threat from carrier aircraft. It was 'Fleet against shore' again, but in this case the Russian shore. It is in the Russian nature to produce layered defence against such threats, so that although they quickly thought in terms of an anti-ballistic missile system and improving their fighter defences, they also tasked the Soviet Navy with countering the vehicles that carried these two threats: that is to say, the Polaris submarines and the United States carriers.

The first was a much tougher problem than the second and the Soviet attempt to manage it will be addressed elsewhere in this book. But a counter even to the aircraft carriers was tough enough.

These big vessels, with complements of nearly 100 aircraft, could deploy a variety of defensive resources and still have plenty left over for striking the mainland. They were supported by substantial escort forces and shore-based maritime patrol aircraft, and they were deployed permanently in the Mediterranean and quite often in the Eastern North Atlantic.

Two components of the Soviet reply, the shore-based missile-armed aircraft and the surface-to-surface missile ships, concern us here only to demonstrate the Soviet preoccupation with an all-arms, co-ordinated response to a major threat. The third component of that response, however, was submarine.

Clearly the main thrust of any torpedo-armed submarine force deployed against fast carrier groups would have to be nuclear-powered; conventional boats would find it hard to achieve, and impossible to maintain, firing positions. It was,

Right:
Near the true submarine shape: the nuclear-powered 'Victor' class. *Crown Copyright*

Below:
A 'Foxtrot' class diesel electric submarine in an uneasy Mediterranean anchorage. Note the snort mast from which the ensign is flying.
Crown Copyright

in any case, in 1958 that the 'November' class nuclear submarine first became available. Its first-generation powerplant and many crudities in its design suggest that it was noisy, none too safe to operate (one sank in the Atlantic in 1970) and lacking in the operational finesse that superior hull form, manoeuvrability and sensors gave to Western boats. But it was there, and it certainly should have given pause to carrier group commanders to know that one was about.

The successor to the 'November' was a much more sophisticated vessel, the 'Victor' class. This was the first Soviet submarine to have a 'tear-drop' hull form with a length-to-beam ratio of well under 10:1. Strength, manoeuvrability and flow are all improved with this sort of hull form and if the 'Victor' is still noisier than contemporary Western boats, as it is reported to be, then it is probably because of inattention to such factors as auxiliary machinery, propeller design and casing holes. The 'Victor' class is certainly armed with torpedoes and is reported to carry the anti-submarine SS-N-15 weapon, tube-launched but airborne for most of its trajectory. If that is so, clearly the class is not only

for use in the anti-carrier role, and further mention will be made of it – particularly the 'Victor III' variant, in rapid production since 1978 – when discussing anti-submarine submarines.

Developments in nuclear-powered torpedo-armed submarines over the last two decades have not meant that the Soviet Union has stopped building conventionally powered boats. The 'Foxtrot' class, a successor to the 'Zulu' rather than the 'Whiskey', came into service in 1958 and the programme was not ended until 1972. They are solid, reliable, unspectacular boats which have given good service and have been sold widely abroad. Mediterranean deployments in particular see many of them; they come down from the Northern Fleet and remain for several months. Armament, so far as is known, consists of torpedoes only. Of course there are torpedoes and torpedoes and there is very little published evidence on how effective the Soviet ones are. It would be surprising if they were very sophisticated – the widespread fitting of nuclear heads suggests that they go for lethal radius rather than pinpoint accuracy – and equally surprising if they were operationally less

Above:
A submarine of the 'Tango' class which succeeded the 'Foxtrot' as the standard Soviet diesel-electric boat. *Crown Copyright*

Below left:
The short-lived successor to the 'Whiskey' class: a 'Romeo' class submarine, of which only 20 were built. *Crown Copyright*

reliable than their Western counterparts. The 'Foxtrot' has in turn been succeeded by the 'Tango' class, which has been in service since 1973 and now totals just under 20 boats. Of similar configuration to the 'Foxtrots', they are smoother, of better hull form and almost certainly quieter. Their very slow building rate, and variations in individual boats, suggest not only a desire to keep the conventionally-

Table 2: Soviet Torpedo-Armed Submarines

				Submarines					**Weapons**	
Number in service	*Class*	*Entered service*	*Propulsion*	*Displacement submerged (tons)*	*Speed submerged (kt)*	*Length (ft)*	*Beam (ft)*		*Torpedo tubes (FWD+aft)*	*Tube-launched ASW weapons*
50 (a)	Whiskey	1951-57	Diesel-electric	1,350	14	249	21		4 + 2	–
8 (b)	Zulu	1951-55	Diesel-electric	2,300	16	295	24		6 + 4	–
12	Romeo	1958-61	Diesel-electric	1,800	14	252	24		6 + 2	–
60	Foxtrot	1958-71	Diesel-electric	2,500	16	300	26		6 + 4	–
13	November	1958-63	Nuclear	5,000	30	360	30		8 + 2	–
5 (c)	Echo I	1960-62	Nuclear	5,200	28	374	30		6 + 2	–
8 (c)	Yankee	1967-74	Nuclear	9,300	30	425	38		6	–
16	Victor I	1968-75	Nuclear	5,200	32	308	33		6	poss SS-N-15
7	Alfa	1970-	Nuclear	3,800	42	260	33		6	SS-N-15
18	Tango	1973-	Diesel-electric	3,700	16	302	30		8	poss SS-N-15
7	Victor II	1976-78	Nuclear	5,800	31	328	33		6	poss SS-N-15
16	Victor III	1978-	Nuclear	6,000	30	341	33		6	SS-N-15
4	Kilo	1982-	Diesel-electric	3,000	18?	220	30?		8?	
1 (d)	Sierra	1984-	Nuclear	8,000	—	360	—		—	SS-N-15
1 (e)	Mike	1984-	Nuclear	9,700	—	360	—		—	SS-N-15

Notes
(a) Many more, possibly 100, in reserve.
(b) Possibly 5 more in reserve.
(c) Missile submarines with tubes removed
(d) Assessed as Victor III successor. Could also carry SS-NX-21 cruise missile for use against land targets.
(e) Assessed as Alfa successor.

powered submarine art alive, but to experiment with it in order to explore its full potential.

These were all ocean-going submarines quite capable of a patrol of three months; indeed, individual boats' peacetime deployments to the Mediterranean have lasted longer, though they do get depot-ship support there in somewhat inhospitable anchorages. Designs of shorter range and endurance were not neglected by the Soviet Navy. The 'Whiskey' was followed in 1958 by the 'Romeo' class, a refined, slightly larger boat that probably was quieter and had better sensors. However this class stopped in 1961 at about 20, of which several were subsequently transferred abroad; and thereafter no medium-range submarines were produced for two decades. It was in 1981 that the first of a new class, the 'Kilo' was seen. This is a boat of some 3,000 tons submerged, but only 220ft long; this implies a very tubby, advanced hull form fully consistent with current Western conventional submarine practice. Although ocean-deployable, it would – will – be a suitable boat for offshore work in the North and the Pacific, and also for the Baltic and Black Seas.

There has, then, been a steady development of torpedo-armed submarines with both nuclear and conventional propulsion, and numbers have been kept up at a level of over 200 boats split among the four fleets. There was enough here to pose a severe threat both to carrier strike forces and to other NATO shipping. However, the Russians are great believers both in numbers and in diversifying the threat; and the possibility of fitting submarines with aerodynamic missiles, for attacking surface ships, gave them the opportunity to do so.

Their first essays in the field were crude. Various modifications of the 'Whiskey' class, carrying anti-ship missiles of several hundred miles' range, appeared in the late 1950s; the tubes were mounted outside the casing, clearly caused flow and possibly stability problems, and entailed surfacing to fire.

Specially designed submarines followed quickly, however. The first to appear, in 1960, was in fact nuclear-powered, though there is some question whether it was the first to be designed. This was the 'Echo' class, a long thin vessel with six (in later models, eight) missiles in paired tubes flush with the casing which elevated to fire. The nuclear propulsion was of the same design as that of the 'November', and the boat had much the same shortcomings of noisiness and doubtful reliability. It had to surface, probably for a considerable time, to fire its missiles. Only a couple of years later the conventionally powered 'Juliett' class began to apppear: built at the Gorki yards 500 miles from the sea, they caused a considerable stir and were in fact quite an achievement, since on a 3,000 ton hull they mounted four missiles and moreover achieved the most advanced hull form of any Soviet submarine up to that time.

For both the 'Echo' and the 'Juliett' classes the missiles were the same. They were small (not very small, at that) pilotless aircraft, with a range of about 250 miles. Launched from the surface on target information from a third party, in those days a reconnaissance aircraft, all but the earliest versions could be given midcourse guidance from the submarine. At a preset distance the missile's active radar terminal homing would take over and the missile would deliver its warhead of 350 kilotons nuclear, or several hundred pounds conventional, explosive.

That was the theory, but there were several drawbacks to the system. The submarine had to be

Below:
A new venture into the small, handy submarine category: the 'Kilo' class, first seen in 1982.
Crown Copyright

Below right:
Beam view of an 'Echo-II' guided missile submarine.
Crown Copyright

Table 3: Soviet Submarines armed with anti-ship missiles

				Submarines				Missiles			
Number in service	Class	Entered service	Propulsion	Displacement submerged (tons)	Speed submerged (kt)	Length (ft)	Beam (ft)	Type	Range (nm)	Launch mode	No of tubes
29	Echo II	1961-67	Nuclear	5,800	25	385	30	SS-N-3 or SS-N-12	250 450	Surfaced Surfaced	8
16	Juliett	1963-68	Diesel-Electric	3,800	14	284	33	SS-N-3 or SS-N-12	250 450	Surfaced Surfaced	4
12	Charlie I	1967-73	Nuclear	5,000	28	308	33	SS-N-7	30	Submerged	8
1	Papa	1971	Nuclear	7,000	35?	357	38	SS-N-9?	150	Submerged	10
6	Charlie II	1972-80	Nuclear	5,500	28	337	33	SS-N-7	30	Submerged	8
2+	Oscar	1981	Nuclear	15,000	?	492	60	SS-N-19	250	Submerged	24

contacted somehow for target data to be passed; the target acquisition unit was certainly vulnerable, so long as aircraft were used for the purpose; the submarine was vulnerable when preparing to fire and during the midcourse guidance phase; the missile was big and flew relatively high, so was detectable; and the homing head could perhaps be seduced or jammed. In fact it posed (and still poses, since some 40 submarines with this armament are in service) a very worrying and widespread threat, but one that gave some chance of being countered, as much or more by air defence measures as by anti-submarine ones.

The next guided missile submarine, the 'Charlie' class, was of a quite different kind. Nuclear-powered and of middling size, it carries eight raked missile tubes in a bulbous bow, from which it can fire, submerged, missiles of much shorter range than those of the 'Echo' and 'Juliett' classes. The clear implication is that this submarine is expected to act in a much more independent way, probably from a shadowing or marking position and firing,

when its rules of engagement allow, on its own sonar data. This poses quite new problems to the target force. In a period of tension, it may detect the 'Charlie' from time to time, but holding contact may not be so easy, and judging any hostile intent on its part more difficult still. Moreover, when the missiles are fired their time of flight will be short and their trajectory could be very low, so they are nothing like so detectable as those from the earlier classes. 18 'Charlies' have been built; one unit of an apparent follow-on class, the 'Papa', appeared 10 years ago, but it looks increasingly as though the operational requirement for this one was not thought through and it may have been shelved on the ground that it fell between the autonomous/short range and reconnaissance-dependent/long range categories.

The second of these categories, having had no representative building since the termination of the 'Echo' and 'Juliett' classes in the late 1960s, has recently acquired a new and very significant member. This is the 'Oscar', the largest anti-ship

Above:
A 'Juliett' class guided missile submarine, with diesel electric propulsion
Crown Copyright

Left:
A 'Charlie' class nuclear-powered submarine, able to fire short-range, sea-skimming anti-ship missiles.
Crown Copyright

submarine ever built, the first of which was launched in 1980. There are more to come. Of 15,000 tons displacement and nearly 500ft long, the 'Oscar' has 24 missile tubes from which it can launch, submerged, missiles of at least 250 nautical miles range. It looks as though at least some of the shortcomings of the earlier long range antiship missile system have now been overcome. For example, target acquisition by satellite may now be much more reliable and communications with the submerged submarine more certain; and the SS-N-19 missiles are probably smaller and fly lower, so decreasing their detectability. Given also the physical toughness such a large double-hulled submarine might expect to have, Western forces are faced with a formidable adversary here.

Submarines for use against submarines

The Russians have not been kind enough to tell us what each of their submarine classes is for. Consequently, when I put only one and a half classes into this section I am making a judgement based on incomplete evidence. It may be that numbers of submarines from the classes just described will be employed, in the event, primarily in the anti-submarine role; it is certain that all their submarines will be alert to the possibility of detecting and destroying an opposing submarine.

whether in self-defence or in the ordinary course of operations. But I do believe that so far as operational requirements go, only the two submarine classes now to be described were conceived as antisubmarine vessels.

The first, in order of laying down, was the 'Alfa' class. In its day – the first was launched in 1970 – this was an exceptionally advanced boat. The hull was constructed of new material, probably titanium alloy, which gave it great strength potential and a theoretical crushing depth of over 2,000ft. It had a new, advanced nuclear powered plant and its speed has been announced by Western official sources as a staggering 42kts. With such performance, it was no wonder that the 'Alfa' class underwent what were apparently severe teething troubles. They are now in slow series production, but still run only to single figures. Operationally their speed and depth clearly pose hard problems to an opposing submarine; there is of course no published information on their

noise signatures, and at high speeds these may be considerable, but such a fast boat could use sprint-and-drift techniques or other dodges, depending on what it was trying to do. That would in turn be governed not only by its sensor capability – on which there is no information – but on its anti-submarine weapons, which include wire-guided torpedoes and the tube-launched SS-N-15 missile. The former could have a range up to 30kms; the latter rather more, with a terminal weapon either of a lightweight homing torpedo or a nuclear depth bomb.

The other submarine that is clearly for anti-submarine work is the third variant of the 'Victor' class. Armed similarly to the 'Alfa', this is a larger, slower boat, having in fact much the same

Fig 1
Soviet submarine forces facing NATO – the general situation. (Serviceability 60-70% of these numbers).

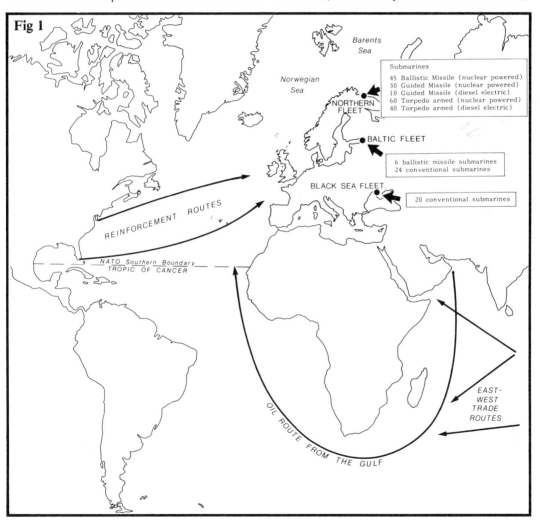

Fig 1

Barents Sea

Norwegian Sea

Submarines
45 Ballistic Missile (nuclear powered)
30 Guided Missile (nuclear powered)
10 Guided Missile (diesel electric)
60 Torpedo armed (nuclear powered)
40 Torpedo armed (diesel electric)

NORTHERN FLEET

BALTIC FLEET

6 ballistic missile submarines
24 conventional submarines

BLACK SEA FLEET

20 conventional submarines

REINFORCEMENT ROUTES

NATO Southern Boundary
TROPIC OF CANCER

OIL ROUTE FROM THE GULF

EAST-WEST TRADE ROUTES

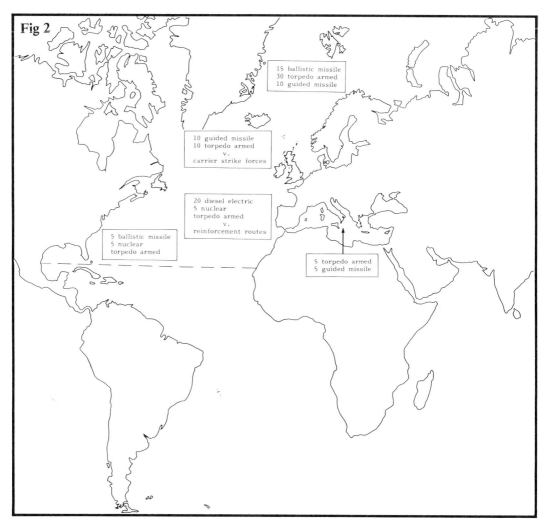

Fig 2

15 ballistic missile
30 torpedo armed
10 guided missile

10 guided missile
10 torpedo armed
v.
carrier strike forces

20 diesel electric
5 nuclear
torpedo armed
v.
reinforcement routes

5 ballistic missile
5 nuclear
torpedo armed

5 torpedo armed
5 guided missile

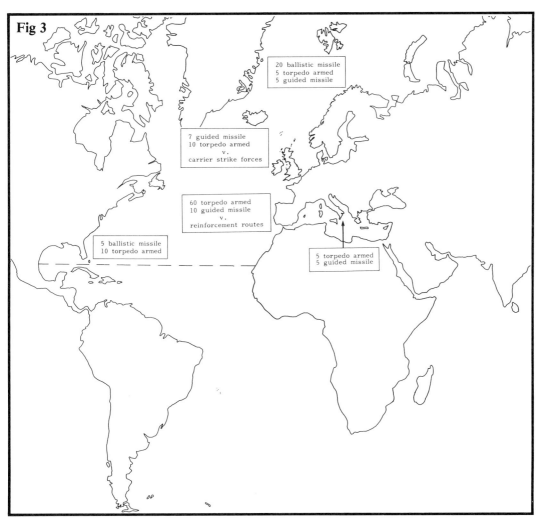

Fig 2
Northern Fleet war deployments: a cautious opinion. The main emphasis is on area defence of the North Norwegian Sea/Barents Sea bastion and preservation of the ballistic missile force.

Fig 3
Northern Fleet war deployment: a large scale anti-shipping campaign. Some predeployment from the Baltic is assumed. There is much more emphasis on countering NATO sea-use of all kinds than in Fig 2.

Left:
The world's fastest submarine, but one that has perhaps cost the Soviet Union a great deal in redevelopment after a disastrous introduction into service: the 'Alfa' class. *Crown Copyright*

characteristics as the previous 'Victor I' and 'Victor II' classes, but with two important differences: a much more streamlined casing, showing great efforts at reducing flow noise, and a large pod mounted on the after fin. This is very probably a towed-array passive sonar, and if so can only be for long range detection of submerged submarines. It is also possible that, like other members of the 'Victor' and 'Alfa' classes, the 'Victor III' has a special coating on its hull to reduce its echoing properties when targeted by active sonar.

Two new classes of submarine have recently been reported. These are the 'Sierra', probably a successor to the 'Victor III', and the 'Mike', probably to succeed the 'Alfa'.

Submarines for inshore operations
There is no current evidence of a Soviet submarine having been constructed specifically for inshore work for nearly 30 years. Then, the 'Quebec' class was undoubtedly designed as a Baltic boat; a few may survive. It would be surprising if some small submersibles did not exist, and there are two

33

Above:
The 'Victor-III' almost certainly has a towed array body housed in the pod on the after fin.
Crown Copyright

submarines, the 'India' class, which carry such vehicles; but of the two that exist, one is based in the Pacific and one in the Northern Fleet, and their primary mission is assessed as submarine rescue.

Of course larger submarines, if they are well-navigated and know the waters, can be used for inshore work. But they are not ideal, and if the Russians do put stress on this role it is surprising that they have not built small handy submarines in considerable numbers. If such a class existed it would certainly be known to the West.

This negative evidence suggests that reports of large numbers of Soviet submarines operating in Scandinavian inshore waters may have to be treated with scepticism. It is not clear in any case why the Soviets would take the political risks involved. The single established violation – the famous 'Whiskey-on-the-Rocks' incident of 1980 – is not evidence of a systematic series of incursions; it could very easily have been a case of a transitting submarine's suffering a combination of low visibility, gyro failure and poorly operated radar to cause a navigational error not uncommon in boats of that generation.

None of this means that the Soviet Navy is incapable of isolated inshore clandestine operations by submarine if a military need is seen.

Soviet submarine deployments and concepts

The Soviet Navy is divided into four fleets: Northern, Baltic, Black Sea and Pacific. The bulk of their submarines, including all the nuclear-powered

ones, are in the fleets that have direct access to the ocean, that is to say the Northern and Pacific. Submarine deployments in peacetime fall into two classes: standing commitments, which appear to be the maintenance of a force level of 10 submarines in the Mediterranean and three in the Indian Ocean plus about a dozen ballistic missile boats on patrol; and exercise and trials commitments, which can vary from upward of 50 submarines for major ocean exercises to isolated and odd goings-on in the North Atlantic. The standing forces in particular can be expected to take great interest in the activities of US carrier groups, and there is evidence, from press reports of Allied prosecution of submarine contacts round western submarine bases, that western ballistic missile submarines are also objects of scrutiny.

The aim of these deployments seems to be to get, and keep, within range of units that are judged to threaten the Soviet home base. Gorshkov is insistent on 'winning the battle for the first salvo'. Against United States carrier groups this aim might quite often be achieved by a combination of guided-missile and torpedo-armed submarines, shadowing or disposed ahead of the force. Against Western ballistic missile boats it is doubtful if it has so far been achieved at all, except perhaps fleetingly on a single unit. Continuous trailing, which is the only way of maintaining contact within firing range, is intrinsically difficult and so far appears quite beyond their capability.

In a period of tension the Soviet Union would probably increase the intensity of such efforts, provided that their strategy allowed them to make such obvious preparatory moves. They would also move submarines into areas of particular sensitivity

Table 4: Non-NATO and Non-Warsaw Pact Submarines

Country		Type	In Service	Displacement Submerged (tons)	Remarks
Albania	3	Whiskey	1958	1,350	ex-Soviet
Argentina	2	Salta	1974	1,285	German built
	1	Guppy	1945	2,540	Ex-US
	2	TR-1700	1984	2,300	German built. 4 more ordered
Australia	6	Oberon	1967-69	2,410	UK built
Brazil	3	Oberon	1973-77	2,410	UK built
	5	Guppy	1945	2,450	Ex-US
Chile	2	Type 209	1984	1,390	German built
	2	Oberon	1976	2,410	UK built
	1	Balao	1944	2,425	Ex-US
China	1+	Xia SSBN	1985?	–	All but the first
	2+	Han SSN	1975	–	5 Whiskeys are
	90	Romeo	1962	1,700	Chinese-built
	21	Whiskey	1957	1,350	
Colombia	2	Type 209	1975	1,285	German built
Cuba	2	Foxtrot	1979	2,500	Ex-Soviet
	1	Whiskey	1979	1,350	Ex-Soviet
Ecuador	2	Type 209	1977	1,285	German built
Egypt	8	Romeo	1966-80	1,700	Ex-Soviet (6) Ex-Chinese (2)
	4	Whiskey	1957-58	1,350	Ex-Soviet
India	2	Type 1500	1984	1,800	German built
	8	Foxtrot	1968-75	2,400	Soviet built. 3 more ordered
Indonesia	4	Type 209	1980-84	1,285	German built
	2	Whiskey	1962	1,350	Ex-Soviet
Israel	3	Type 206	1977	600	UK built
Japan	7	Yuushio	1980-85	2,200	
	7	Uzushio	1971-78	1,850	
	4	Asashio	1966-69	1,600	
Korea North	14	Romeo	1973-78	1,700	7 built in China
	4	Whiskey	1965	1,350	Ex-Soviet
Libya	5	Foxtrot	1976-83	2,400	Soviet built
Pakistan	2	Agosta	1979	1,725	French built
	4	Daphne	1970	1,045	French built
Peru	6	Type 1200	1974-82	1,290	German built
	4	Abtao	1954-57	1,400	US built
	2	Guppy	1944	2,440	Ex-US
South Africa	3	Daphne	1970	1,045	French built
Sweden	4	A17	1985	–	
	3	Näcken	1980	1,125	
	5	Sjöormen	1968	1,400	
	4	Draken	1962	1,110	
Taiwan	2	Guppy	1945	2,420	Ex-US. Two further submarines ordered from Netherlands
Venezuela	4	Type 209	1976-83	1,390	German built
	1	Guppy	1951	2,420	Ex-US
Yugoslavia	2	Sava	1978	965	
	3	Heroj	1969	1,070	
	2	Sutjeska	1961	945	

to the USSR: the Norwegian Sea and the Seas of Japan and Okhotsk. These would cater for what has been called the 'encounter battle'; the Soviets tend to use phraseology drawn from land warfare. More submarines would be deployed closer to their own ballistic missile boats in order to protect them against the threat of attack. And finally, some submarines would be sent out to disrupt Western shipping traffic on the so-called Sea Lines of Communication.

Most experts would probably agree that the main functions of Soviet submarines in war are as the previous paragraph describes them. The critical question is: how will the effort be distributed? Will the Soviets be so obsessed with the threat to the USSR that they throw most of their effort against Western strike forces, even trying desperately to chase Western ballistic missile submarines? Or will they pay disproportionate attention to a threat to their own ballistic missile submarines in the Barents Sea 'bastion', putting all their newest and best nuclear boats into the defence? Or will they concentrate on disrupting reinforcement shipping across the Atlantic?

The West's predictions of Soviet plans and the dispositions it makes itself in order not only to protect its interests but to channel the battle in the way that suits it best, could well be critical to the outcome – if it ever comes to that. One must not forget, however, that in Western doctrine the main business of readiness for war is not to fight wars, but to deter them. Proper Western provision against every contingency, with never the possibility of a free ride for the opponent, is the best safeguard.

Other Submarine Threats

In his famous book 'Gunboat Diplomacy', Sir James Cable counted 131 cases between 1947 and 1979 in which naval force or the threat of naval force were used coercively in disputes around the world.

Below:
The Argentine submarine *Salta*. Many submarines of this size and capability have been supplied to nations which belong neither to NATO nor to the Warsaw Pact. *Crown Copyright*

In the summaries appended to his table, every sort of maritime unit is mentioned except submarines. (The word 'submarine' occurs once – in connection with the cutting of a submarine cable!) There is no coincidence in the omission; analysis of recent history, and argument from first principles, both suggest that the submarine is unlikely to be chosen as a tool of limited naval force, and has very seldom been so chosen. Therefore, if the right measures are taken to ensure that sea-based disputes – of which there will be no fewer round the world in future – are settled before they escalate into open warfare, the threat from opposing submarines will be more potential than actual.

Once conflict assumes the character of war, however, submarines are less subject to constraint and I think that states will tend to be less reluctant to use them after the experience of the Indo-Pakistan war of 1971, when one Indian frigate was sunk by a submarine and one Pakistani submarine by surface forces, and of the South Atlantic campaign of 1982, when HMS *Conqueror* sank the Argentine cruiser *General Belgrano* and Argentina claimed that one of its submarines operated against the British Task Force.

It would be invidious to pick out any particular non-NATO navies as threats in the context of sea-based disputes in future. History shows that almost any country, however basically friendly, can become an opponent over a particular issue, and that if badly handled such conflicts can lead to shooting. Round the world, there are 23 non-NATO and non-Warsaw Pact navies that possess submarines. Generally speaking, each nation possesses under 10, though of course China has many more including at least two with nuclear power. Apart from that, all submarines at present are conventionally powered and torpedo-armed, and many are small coastal types. This is not necessarily good news for anti-submarine forces. Such small craft, though of limited endurance, are intrinsically difficult to detect, particularly as many are modern and quiet, and they may be operating in waters they know and where the sonic conditions make detection unusually difficult. But for a better understanding of these matters, it is necessary to read the next chapter.

The Means

The aim of anti-submarine warfare is to deny to the enemy the effective use of his submarines. This can be done both by destroying those submarines, and by adopting dispositions, movements and tactics that inhibit them. This chapter will discuss both methods, and indeed combinations of them; if it pays more attention to the first than to the second, it does so not only because it is more exciting to read about, but because it is the more decisive and the one that absorbs more resources.

Submarines can, of course, sometimes be destroyed in their bases or building yards by aerial attack or by sabotage. Those methods do not fall within the scope of this book; it is necessary only to make the point that they depend on political approval to carry the conflict on to the enemy's land territory, even more critically so if nuclear attacks are involved; that such locations are likely to be physically protected and heavily defended; and that many submarines will already be at sea. Campaigns of this sort, may, therefore, be useful in helping to achieve the anti-submarine aim, but they will not be the whole answer.

The detection and destruction of submarines at sea, then, will be the main subject-matter of this chapter. As has already been suggested, the more modern submarines have tended to carry the problem down, away from the interface and into the depths; and so it is pre-eminently with detection and destruction in the sea, rather than at the surface, that we are concerned.

The Ancient Greeks weren't idiots, and when they called earth, water and air 'elements' they were reflecting the very different characters, and governing physical laws, of the states of matter. They would have understood at once that detecting a fully-submerged submarine is a quite different problem from detecting one that exposes part of itself above the surface. They would certainly have understood better than the BBC newswriter who claimed, early in 1983, that a submarine alleged to be lying on the bottom of a Norwegian fjord had been detected by radar.

For of course radar, which uses waves in the electromagnetic spectrum, has virtually no penetration under water. Wireless waves of very low frequency can do rather better, to a few hundred feet perhaps; and there is a so-called 'blue-green window' where the particular properties of laser-generated light in a certain frequency band might be harnessed to achieve similar penetrations. But the potential of both these principles seems to be limited to communication only. For a means of finding submerged submarines, it is necessary to turn to another form of wave energy: sound.

The Sonic Environment

A submarine can be detected acoustically in two ways. First, a listening device may hear sounds emitted by the submarine: noise caused by the formation and collapse of bubbles as it, and its propellers, pass through the water; noise caused by

Below:
Passive sonar sensors: a rack of Jezebel sonobuoys in a helicopter. *Crown Copyright*

Fig 4

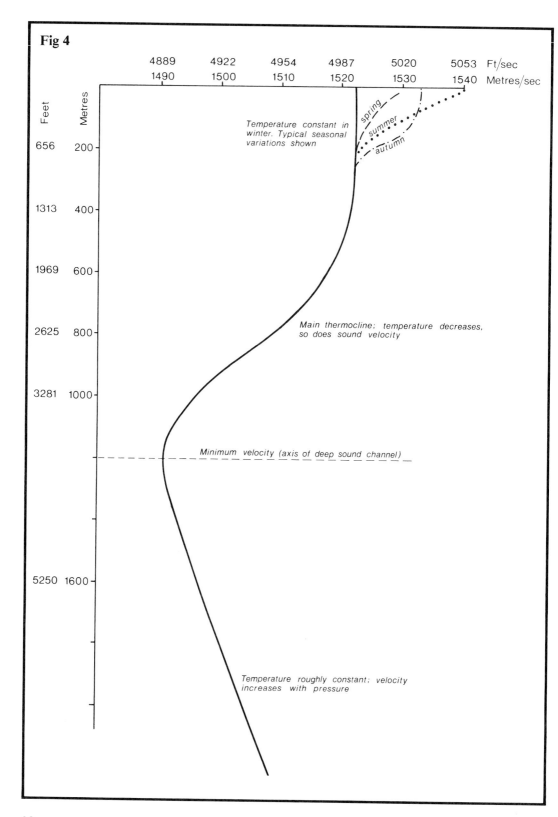

the more regular pulsations of its internal machinery; noise caused by transmissions on the submarine's own sonic systems; noise sometimes, even, caused by injudicious actions of the command or the crew (try dropping a teacup in the ultra-quiet state and see how popular you are). Listening for submarine-generated noise in this way is called passive sonar. Second, a device may be used to transmit powerful pulses of sound, which are reflected by large bodies in the sea (including submarines) and can then be picked up by an associated receiver either in the transmitting unit or, less frequently, elsewhere. This is active sonar.

Sound travels quite well, but very unevenly, through water; and both passive and active sonar performance are greatly affected by the anomalies of its passage.

First, and most important, a ray of sound seldom travels in a straight line through the sea. Through a homogeneous body of water, it would; but the sea is not homogeneous. Its temperature, pressure and salinity all vary at different points, and particularly at different depths; since the velocity of sound in the sea varies with all these factors, and since with change of velocity there is a change in the direction of the ray, the bending effects are considerable and cannot be eradicated.

Let us take this a little further, for it critically affects not only the effectiveness of sonar but all anti-submarine operations that are sonar-dependent. A typical column of water in the open ocean has a structure in which salinity does not vary significantly and pressure increases with depth; temperature follows a much more variable pattern, but the most common consists of a belt of water down to a few hundred feet in which the temperature is more or less constant, followed by a drop in temperature over the next few thousand feet (this is called the 'permanent thermocline') followed by near-constant temperature again down to the bottom. The effect on sound velocity is that it is fairly constant in the near-surface belt, so sound rays do not get bent too much; after that it decreases with depth, so a sound ray is bent progressively downwards; but at 4,000ft or so the velocity begins to increase with pressure, and the effect is to start bending sound rays up again.

In this classic case, then, there is a surface duct where sound will travel to and fro pretty well, finally petering out when it has encountered too many water molecules (which absorb its energy and turn it into heat) or pieces of marine life (which do the same only more so). But underneath this duct sound will not go very far before it is bent downwards, causing a shadow zone where neither an emitter nor a reflector of sound can readily be detected by an observer in the duct. At a certain depth, however – the depth of minimum velocity, or the axis of the deep sound channel – sound will be focused and will tend to return to the surface, so that objects in its path may once more be detected, this time by a ray that has followed a kind of skipping path. Typically, such detections occur in what are called the convergence zones at about 30 and again at about 60 miles from the observer.

The last two paragraphs may have seemed complicated but in fact they were grossly simplified. The layer of water between the surface and the start of the permanent thermocline is often subject to temperature variations that cause shadow zones much closer to the surface than in the classical case.

Fig 4
Variation of sound velocity with depth

Below:
Active sonar operators in a frigate.
Crown Copyright

Below right:
The PMS-26 small ship active sonar with its single operator. *The Plessey Co Ltd*

These are the sort of conditions found in the Mediterranean in summer, where the surface duct is warm and very shallow indeed, and a sharp negative gradient beneath it causes massive propagation losses against targets at depths of little more than 100ft. Again, shallow water will produce effects far removed from the classical case; it stands to reason that a bottom shallower than the deep sound channel will seriously disrupt the pattern that has been described. In fact a bottom that is a good reflector may help to achieve remarkable skip effects; the difficulty will be to predict them. Other variations, such as freshets in coastal water or diurnal changes in the temperature and the level at which the main biomass of small sea creatures places itself, can cause quite sharp changes in sonar performance even in the same place and with the same sonar outfit.

From all this, two conclusions are clear. First, however difficult it is to know what is going on in this imperfectly understood medium – the sea – the anti-submarine practitioner must make every effort to gather all the relevant data and keep it up to date, hour by hour, minute by minute, and use it to its fullest extent. Without it he is lost. Second, the depth at which sensors are placed, or can by their design be placed, is of critical importance. So of course is the depth at which opposing submarines are operated; and the bathymetric contest is just as important now as the struggle for the weather-gauge used to be in the days of sail.

It is not, of course, only the relative depths of the

Above:
The bow sonar dome of USS *Ticonderoga*. *General Electric Corp*

Fig 5
Formation of shadow and convergence zones.

Fig 6
Bottom effects and sonars below the layer.

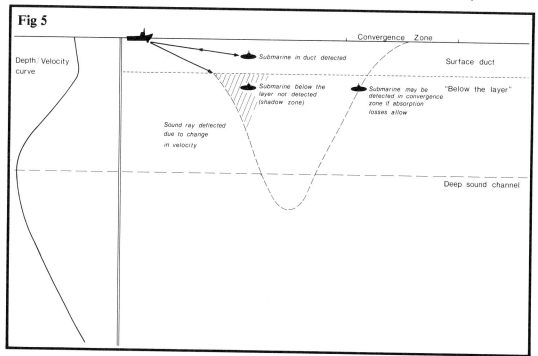

Fig 5

Depth/Velocity curve

Convergence Zone

Submarine in duct detected

Surface duct

Submarine below the layer not detected (shadow zone)

Submarine may be detected in convergence zone if absorption losses allow

"Below the layer"

Sound ray deflected due to change in velocity

Deep sound channel

target and the sonar set, in the conditions of the moment, that will govern the distance at which a submarine is detected. For passive sonars, a critical factor is the frequency of the noises emitted by the target. Flow and cavitation noise – the formation and collapse of the bubbles – occurs over a wide range of frequencies, and is generally called broadband noise. The noise from machinery has a more regular beat, often of only a few cycles a second (Hertz) and is therefore, typically, not only of narrow bandwidth but of low frequency. The value of this to the detector is twofold: it is readily identifiable by passive sonar processing equipment; and it suffers less attenuation than higher-frequency sound, that is to say that the lower the frequency of a sound of a given intensity, the further off it can be heard. Finally, active sonar transmissions from a submarine can be heard by anti-submarine forces, but for that very reason prudent submariners are very sparing in their use. If the would-be detector hears one of those, he is lucky.

Active sonars for detection are subject to the same physical laws, though of course the sound is affected throughout its two-way trip, and what is more a lot gets lost on reflection from the target, so propagation losses are relatively severe. If one wants a long range for a given power emission, one had better make the frequency as low as possible. But technically, it is not so easy then to focus the beam down a single bearing and so accuracy may be lost. Nor will the great advantage of active over passive sonar – the ability, through the measurement of time-difference between transmission and reception of the echo, to derive an accurate range – be quite so marked at low frequencies because of the somewhat spread-out transmission pulse. Finally, of course, the emitted power will be an important determinant of detection range, because the more energy that is pushed out, the greater will be the reflected signal. Unfortunately the relation is not linear, so an increase in power does not produce a proportionate increase in range.

Finally, a number of external factors govern detection performance. Both passive and active sonars are adversely affected if they are moving fast through the water and generating their own flow noise. If near the surface, they may move up and down too, with consequent squelching and further degradation. Then, of course, the sea has a lot of inhabitants other than submarines. Passive sonar will hear all the noises made by surface ships, sea creatures, weather and undersea volcanic activity. Its processing systems are designed specially to separate out and identify noise that may come from a submarine, but the more sensitive the receiver the more sophisticated these must be. Active sonar may receive very submarine-like echoes from large sea creatures, and picking out a faint submarine echo from the reverberations, including bottom reflections, that are a constant background to the sonar display is a difficult process. Therefore, with both passive and active sonars, false alarms are a problem, and a problem moreover which tends to

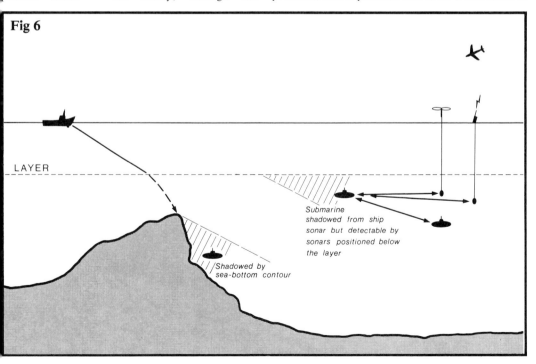

Fig 6

LAYER

Submarine shadowed from ship sonar but detectable by sonars positioned below the layer

Shadowed by sea-bottom contour

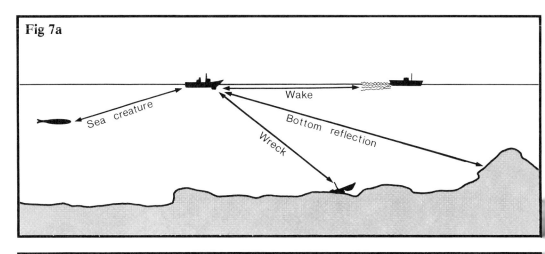

Fig 7a

Sea creature

Wake

Bottom reflection

Wreck

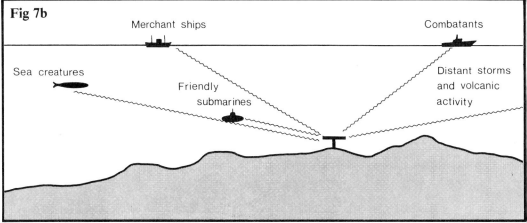

Fig 7b

Merchant ships

Combatants

Sea creatures

Friendly
submarines

Distant storms
and volcanic
activity

increase the more powerful and sensitive the equipment becomes.

Non-Acoustic Detection

Anything as big, solid and mobile as a submarine is bound to do several things, beyond making a noise, to the area through which it passes. Because it is made of ferrous metal, it will cause a local change in the earth's magnetic field. Because its machinery needs cooling, it will take in circulating water and discharge it at a higher temperature. Because it displaces water as it moves, it will set up turbulence both vertically and horizontally. Because it has a human crew, it generates waste products that have to be discharged from time to time. By disturbing small bioluminiscent sea creatures, it may sometimes cause a visible trail. Radioactivity, and heat anomalies apart from circulating water, are confined within the submarine's powerplant and hull, respectively, and can be discounted.

There is considerable interest in the USA in these aspects, particularly as to whether the Soviet Union, which is known to have done research on

Fig 7
Sonar – interference from non-submarine objects: (a) active; (b) passive.

Fig 8
Non-acoustic submarine effects: (a) fully submerged; (b) periscope depth.

Right:
Radar can still be a useful sensor against conventional submarines and deters too free a use of the periscope: the radar screen is seen at the bottom of the picture. *Crown Copyright*

non-acoustic detection methods, has made significant progress in any of them. It is generally agreed, of course, that the magnetic effect can be detected at distances of several hundred feet; Magnetic Anomaly Detectors (MAD) are in use in Western and Eastern maritime air forces. But they are not long-range devices. For the rest of the non-acoustic methods, the main problem is to separate out those effects that are caused by a submarine from those that occur naturally. An omniscient

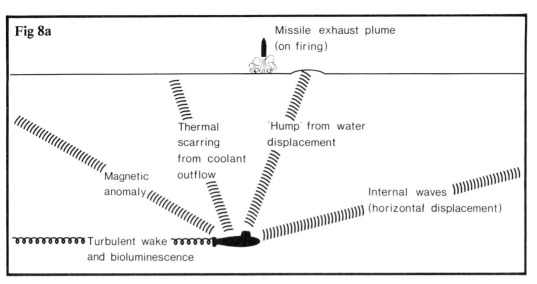

Fig 8a

Missile exhaust plume
(on firing)

Thermal
scarring
from coolant
outflow

'Hump' from water
displacement

Magnetic
anomaly

Internal waves (horizontal displacement)

Turbulent wake
and bioluminescence

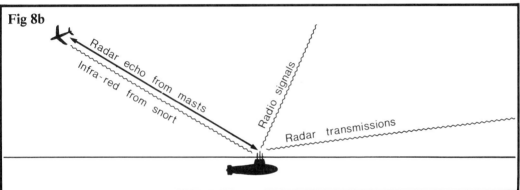

Fig 8b

Radar echo from masts

Infra-red from snort

Radio signals

Radar transmissions

computer linked to an all-observing satellite could, no doubt, do the job; but it looks as though the degrees of both knowledge and observation that would be needed are many orders of magnitude beyond what can be achieved, even in the case of the so-called 'thermal scarring' at the sea's surface which is probably the effect that promises most success. So, while it is important to keep an eye on the possibility of developments in this field, the operational effect both now and in the next decade must be regarded as negligible.

There is, of course, a range of detection methods available against a submarine that pokes anything above the surface. Even an attack periscope can be detected by a modern airborne radar at distances of well over 10 miles. Radar, and conventional radio, transmissions from submarines can be detected, and their bearings obtained. Infra-red detection of exhaust plumes from missiles, once fired, may provide a datum. The snort mast of a conventional submarine provides both a radar and an infra-red target, and in normal operations such submarines need to snort for several hours in the 24.

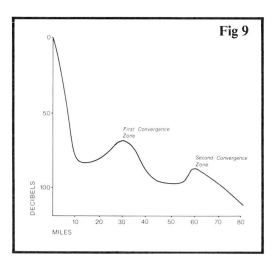

Fig 9

DECIBELS

0

50

First Convergence Zone

Second Convergence Zone

100

MILES

10   20   30   40   50   60   70   80

Fig 9
Decibels and Propagation Losses
Because sound varies so very widely in intensity, and because comparison between one level of sound and another, rather than comparison with any absolute level, is most useful for ASW, logarithmic units are normally employed for measurement. The formula is $N = 10 \log_{} I_1/I_2$ where N is the difference in decibels between two sounds of intensity I_1 and I_2. Being interpreted this means for example that a sound of 30db is 1,000 times stronger than unit intensity; or again, that when a sound source is said to be 20db stronger than another, the sound from the first source is 100 times stronger than the second.
I hope that's clear. The graph shows typical propagation loss of a sound of unit intensity as range from the sound increases.

The Anti-Submarine Process

Finding a submerged submarine, then, is largely an acoustical business and depends on a combination of a large number of factors. Some years ago it was fashionable to talk about the 'sonar equation' particularly in comparisons of Allied and Warsaw Pact submarines, expressing their emitted noise and passive-sonar sensitivity in terms of the one being a number of decibels 'down' on the other. For one-to-one encounters of unalerted submarines both being operated at their optimum, this notion may have some validity; for the more complex interactions that are likely to occur in real life, it is misleading.

The fact is that even as it concerns a single target submarine, the anti-submarine process is likely to involve several units. Whether that happens, or whether a single unit carries it through to completion, it will go through five phases: Detection, Classification, Localisation, Tracking and Kill. Some writers on ASW telescope some of these: I prefer not to, for reasons which will become clear.

Detection

Detection means that *something has been observed which may be a submarine*. This chapter has already dwelt for some time on the nature of detections. They may be characteristic sounds heard on passive sonar, echoes on active sonar, radar contacts which could be snorts or periscopes, intercepts of submarine transmissions, sightings by that usually reliable sensor the eye, or (all too often) an otherwise unexplainable explosion in a ship in company.

A passive acoustic detection may come from a variety of sources. There is a by now widely publicised system of bottom-array hydrophones, backed by very sophisticated shore processing equipment, called SOSUS, which covers the Northern Fleet approaches and the deeper parts of

the North Atlantic. Rapidly-deployable back-up systems are becoming available. A number of surface ships and submarines can now be fitted with towed hydrophone arrays covering an impressive frequency range. Submarines not so fitted still have a considerable passive capability from hull-mounted hydrophones. Aircraft, both fixed and rotary wing, can drop sonobuoys and monitor the acoustic fields thus created. And special ASW mines can gain passive detection on submarines that pass close to them. That catalogue was in descending order of range capability; sonobuoys cannot be expected to be as sensitive as very large bottom arrays.

Active acoustic detections are likely to come either from heavy helicopters carried in medium-sized or large ships, or from surface warships. This is not because other units do not have active sonar, but because passive is their preferred search mode.

Below:
Inboard end of the American TACTAS passive sonar towed array. *Gould Inc*

Right:
A principal platform for active sonar: the Sea King HAS 2 about to dip. *Crown Copyright*

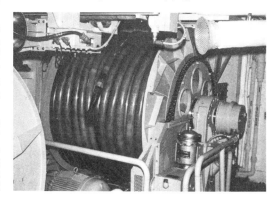

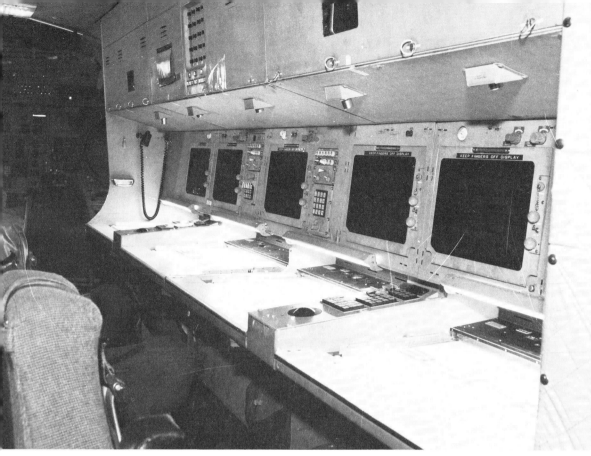

Above-water detections may come from a variety of units: aircraft are the best platforms for periscope-detecting radar, ships may intercept submarine radar transmissions and shore stations have been successful in the past in gaining information from submarine radio transmissions.

Classification

Sometimes a detection is unquestionably a submarine. But, in most cases, it is necessary to come to *a judgement about the nature of the contact*: that is what classification means. If a non-submarine contact is incorrectly classified as a submarine and prosecuted, it will certainly waste anti-submarine forces' time, and probably ammunition as well. If a submarine contact is incorrectly classified as non-submarine, it will survive to do who knows what damage. Nor, historically, are wrong classifications at all rare. Exercises in the 1950s, with sonar operators inexperienced in war conditions, regularly in the writer's experience turned up false alarm rates of over 50%, as well as quite a number of genuine detections which were classified as non-submarine. Even with modern aids, the task of classification is still by no means easy.

Passive sonar processing equipment seeks to separate out, and if possible enhance, submarine-generated sound from all the other whoops, gurgles,

clicks, honks and hisses that are going on in the sea at the same time. It does this by the application of a technique that used to be (and so far as I know still is) called Fast Fourier Transforms. This uses the ability of modern electronic circuitry to scan inputs very rapidly – several thousand times a second. By this means the randomly occurring noises, of each frequency, are filtered out while the consistently occurring ones, such as may be made by a submarine are retained. But of course interpretation by the operator is still needed to assess whether it is in fact a submarine, or some other vessel, or a passing phenomenon; and the lower the ratio of the signal to the ambient noise, the more difficult the problem is, so classification at extreme ranges will take longer and be less certain.

Classification of active sonar contacts used to be the acme of the anti-submariner's art. I recall one commanding officer who donned the headphones at the start of an exercise and took them off only to go below at infrequent intervals between that moment and the one when 'Exercise Completed' was signalled up to a fortnight later. He would start up from sleep crying 'That's a submarine!' as some faint echo, barely distinguishable from the surrounding reverberations, was heard; and he was more often right than wrong. He couldn't explain how he knew: 'It's a metallic sound' was the nearest he came. Such aural skills are still in demand, but signal analysis and its presentation on visual displays is increasingly called in aid. Two techniques are employed: the use of the well-known Doppler Effect, where an approaching target will, because of its relative movement, return an echo of higher frequency than the background reverberations; and digital analysis of the actual shape of an echo returned by a target, so that some estimate of length and inclination can be made. The operators of modern sonars that use either of these techniques are quietly confident of their ability to classify contacts correctly. One hopes they are right; and that they still have the earphones handy, particularly in difficult water conditions.

Even above-water sightings are subject to error. The radar echo that's detected for one sweep only:

is it a cautious submariner's attack periscope taking a quick look, or a gannet's beak at a particular angle of incidence? The young lookout's periscope sighting: what happened to that broom-handle ditched by the Screen Commander's ship 20 minutes ago? So it goes, too, for electronic indications. As has been said before, the more sensitive the equipment, the higher the false alarm rate will intrinsically be, and the greater the amount of filtering that is needed.

Contacts are classified according to a simple code that lays the classifier's judgement on the line.

Left:
Cathode-ray and hard-copy presentation of passive sonar data for both detection and classification. AQS-901 installation in the Nimrod Mk 2.
Marconi Avionics Ltd

Right:
Classification of active sonar contacts: a doppler display is valuable. *The Plessey Co Ltd*

Below:
Signal analysis is another aid to classification: Type 2016 computer room in HMS *Broadsword*.
The Plessey Company Limited

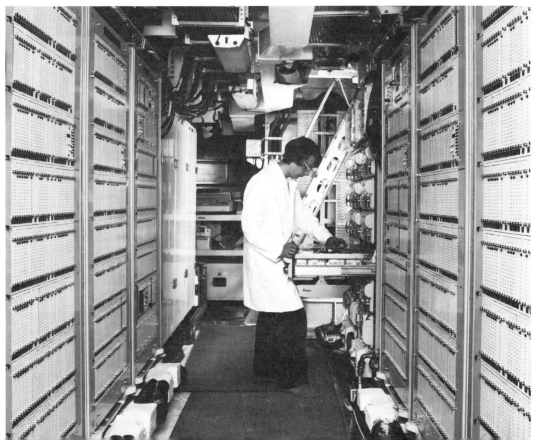

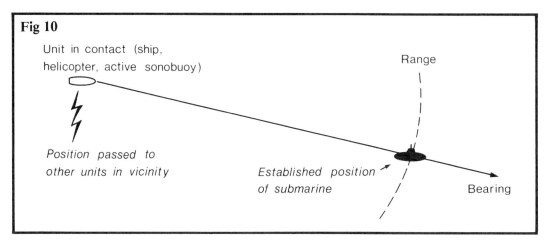

Fig 10

Unit in contact (ship, helicopter, active sonobuoy)

Range

Position passed to other units in vicinity

Established position of submarine

Bearing

Fig 10
Acoustic localisation: active sonar

Right:
Clear enough in the picture, but snorts and periscopes are not easily classifiable if detected by radar or by eye at extreme range. *Crown Copyright*

CERTSUB means there is no doubt: an authenticated sighting, a torpedoing. PROBSUB means there are strong indications that the contact is a submarine. POSSUB means that it may be a submarine; it shows certain submarine characteristics; if in a threatening position, it may be worth prosecuting.

Localisation
First indications of a submarine may give only the vaguest of positions. For instance, a NATO report published in 1982 said that SOSUS was capable of fixing the position of a submarine 'within 50 miles'; and it is well known that a single passive sonar, whether ship, submarine or sonobuoy deployed, can give only a bearing initially. After development of the contact for some time, including analysis of the bearing movement, the detecting unit may come up with an estimated range but this will never be more than an estimate; for a fix, a cross-bearing from at least one other passive sonar is needed. Active sonar comes much nearer to giving an accurate position with a single contact, but even this means requires a few moments' resolution and active sonar ranges are, of course, generally of a lower order than passive ones.

The name of the process of *arriving at an accurate position for a submarine contact* is localisation. If anyone thinks this an Americanism, they should know that it is used in a British Admiralty report of 1917 on 'The Behaviour of Sea-Lions towards Subaqueous Sounds'. Down, Towser! Acoustically, localisation is most often accomplished either by active sonar, which once in firm contact will give a range and bearing from the transmitting unit, generating a position that can then be related to the positions of all other interested units; or, less certainly and accurately, by integrating the responses from several passive sonars, either by cross-bearings if those sonars generate bearing information or by comparison of signal strengths if, as in the case of non-directional sonobuoys, they do not. A special case of localisation is relocation: in this case, a submarine contact on which indications are no longer available or are very tenuous is investigated by a unit, often an aircraft, specially tasked to do so. The aircraft is likely to search round a datum established for it by the appropriate authority, who may be in a ship, or ashore, or in another aircraft, and will use either sonobuoys or dunking sonar. If it gains contact and classifies the contact as POSSUB or higher, it can of course report the position to all units in the vicinity. Accurate navigation by all the units involved is a prerequisite of this technique.

Localisation may also be achieved by magnetic anomaly detector (MAD), generally carried by aircraft. But the short range of MAD entails flying close to the submarine and this could alarm it, so aircrew are chary of using MAD except as a last-minute confirmation before attack or just after it. It is also possible to localise by a visual or radar sighting, but localisations of this sort will usually be fleeting.

Tracking
If a submarine is localised by a unit and localisation is continued at known intervals, a track is generated; the submarine's past movements can be displayed and its future movements, perhaps, predicted. It is therefore possible to think of tracking simply as a subset of localisation, and many ASW pundits do not separate the two.

However, I prefer to, because tracking has a specific purpose that localisation does not, and because a single localisation, or a sporadic set of localisations, will not fulfil it. The purpose is simply

to carry on the ASW process to a point where a kill can be attempted. Tracking, therefore, is *the generation of an estimate of a submarine's past and future movement that will enable a fire control solution to be worked out.*

Tracking can be achieved even by non-directional passive sonars, provided that there are enough of them, that they are cleverly placed and used, and that their performance is consistent. For example, the Doppler Effect can be harnessed to judge the moment at which a submarine passes closest to a sonobuoy; the frequency of a particular spectral line of sound will drop as it does so, and a good operator who knows his equipment may manage an accurate estimate of this closest point of approach. He will also, of course, establish a true frequency for each spectral line, and this will serve as a base for

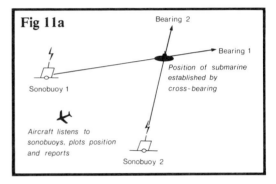

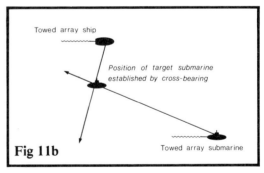

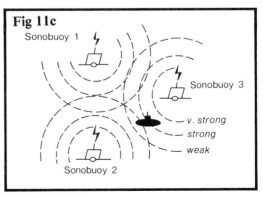

Fig 11
Acoustic localisation: passive sonar.
(a) By directional sonobuoys. Note: accuracy depends on accuracy of both bearings. A third is needed to confirm.
(b) By directional arrays. Note: Positions of detecting units relative to target and to each other are critical to get good angle of cut. Good communications between surface ship and towed array submarine are essential.
(c) By non-directional sonobuoys. Note: strong signal from Sonobuoy 3, weak from Sonobuoy 2, none from Sonobuoy 1, places submarine at location indicated. But accuracy depends on consistent sonobuoy performance.

comparison when further sonobuoys are laid and respones obtained from them.

Clearly, though, this sort of tracking is a constantly-refined series of estimates. A track generated from positions obtained by steadily updated cross-bearings from directional passive sensors will be more precise, more accurate so long as the bearings are accurate and 'cut' at a broad angle, and more amenable to processing by computer.

However, generally speaking a fire control solution is more comfortably achieved by the sort of tracking of which active sonar is alone capable: a steady updating of both range and bearing from the same unit. In these conditions, alterations of course and speed by the target submarine are much more readily detected and predictions about its future movements less difficult.

Although active sonobuoys are available, the more reliable active sonars are in either surface ships or helicopters, and this makes them valuable vehicles for providing fire control solutions.

Some authorities have suggested that one submarine could track another continuously at close quarters by means of precise active sonar. They add that if the technique was used against ballistic

missile submarines, the stability of strategic deterrence would suffer. My own view is that it is very doubtful if the process could be carried on for hours or days, as these commentators suggest. But, of course, submarines are eminently capable of reaching fire control solutions on submarine targets of opportunity.

The possibility of tracking for short periods by radar or visual means should not be discounted. It presupposes a certain lack of alertness in the target submarine, but submarines are not always alert; in World War 2, many were surprised on the surface, and even in what are evidently meant to be realistic exercise conditions, Soviet submarine sightings are not uncommon.

Kill

In order to kill a submerged submarine, it is necessary *to put into the water a weapon that will explode within a lethal radius* from it. Several factors militate against success. First, lethal radii, for charges or warheads of conventional explosive, are tens of feet at most. Second, there will be a time delay, between the release of the weapon and the time it explodes, made up of the time of flight through the air and time in the water. During this 'dead time' the target may alter course, speed or depth. Finally, the target position is subject to errors in computation in the directing unit, and when another unit is involved as a weapon carrier the errors are likely to be compounded.

Several methods are available to minimise these factors. The most obvious is to increase the lethal radius, and the most obvious way of doing that is to employ a nuclear depth bomb. The lethal radius of such devices is classified, but can be expected to be several orders of magnitude greater than high explosive. The difficulties, of course, lie in obtaining political clearance – which is not likely to be granted so long as the conflict has remained conventional – and in any danger to one's own forces in the vicinity.

A second way of improving one's chances is to minimise the time of flight. The old-fashioned, free-falling depth charge, particularly if delivered by aircraft, could be the best bet here. Sinking time, of course, must still be taken into account; but plastering the sea with patterns of depth charges,

Right:
The humble depth charge, still a common and useful anti-submarine weapon. *Crown Copyright*

Below:
Of longer range than the depth charge but still with a relatively short 'dead time': the Limbo anti-submarine mortar. (Photo by C.P.O. Drew).
Crown Copyright

though crude, might turn out to be a much more common feature of any future conflict than tactical sophisticates now seem to believe. What does not kill may still scare or damage, and in war that too has value.

The solution most in favour in the West at present, however, is clearly the intelligent weapon. The principle behind this is that so long as it is put into the water within a certain distance from the target, such a weapon will itself be able to refine target position enough to home on to the target, and indeed to attack it at a vulnerable spot. The terminal weapon in this solution is always an acoustic-headed torpedo. Delivered to the target area either by parachute from an aircraft, or air-flight missile from a ship or submarine, the torpedo searches in passive or active mode and, having acquired the target, homes on to it. A variation on this theme is the submarine-fired wire-guided torpedo; this weapon is in the water throughout its travel, being kept under control by the firing submarine until it is within detection range by its own sensors, when it is released to make its terminal run. These last weapons have two advantages: not being airborne weapons they have far fewer weight limitations, so potentially can carry better propulsion and sensors

and a bigger warhead; and their guidance in mid-course by the parent submarine, which is continuously tracking the target, theoretically reduces the 'dead time' to zero. The main doubt about this solution concerns the reliability of the torpedo. The torpedo's track record, as a ready weapon at the start of conflict, is appalling; German, American and British torpedoes all performed badly at the start of World War 2, and the more intelligent they tried to be, the worse they performed. Comprehensive and stringent trials, and great attention to preparation of outfits in combatant units, are necessary to ensure an acceptable success rate with any torpedo system.

Putting it together

Each individual anti-submarine process, then, is a path with many pitfalls and points of doubt where it is easy to go astray. Put together, all these individual processes constitute an anti-submarine campaign. The challenge facing the planners is to provide the tactical concepts and resources that will enable a successful anti-submarine campaign to be fought (and will, therefore, deter a rational opponent from regarding submarine warfare as a desirable option) while at the same time achieving the use of the sea that their overall strategy requires.

Planning, therefore, will involve working out what use of the sea one is hoping to make; what submarine measures the opponent is most likely to take to frustrate this use; what balance of anti-submarine assets is most likely to deny him the effective use of his submarines; and how those assets are to be most efficiently used. It can be seen at once that all these factors interact, and the planning has to be recycled before coming – one hopes – to a satisfactory conclusion. There are several powerful constraints at work throughout this recycling: the two most important are money, which will always be short, and development inertia, which is simply a pretentious way of saying that a weapon or system project that is nine-tenths of the way to production cannot readily be scrapped in favour of something a bit better.

Striking the right balances is the core of the planning problem. Since technology and tactics interact so much it is a toss-up where one starts. But let us think about the technological balances first.

Material Considerations

A balance must be struck between passive and active acoustic, and non-acoustic, sensing methods. There is no doubt where the greatest advances have been made since World War 2; passive systems have not only made great strides in the ranges they can achieve but have come through very strongly as classification devices. By contrast, active sonars are still more sensitive to the workings of the laws of physics, and have moreover the disadvantages of acting as beacons for eagerly listening submarines. On the other hand, active sonars are more sure providers of precise information at the sharp end of the anti-submarine process; you may kill some submarines with passive only, but you will kill more if you go active. The place of non-acoustic methods is certainly at the detection end of the process, and varies between relatively simple old-established methods–the radar and the lookout–and entirely novel and far-fetched ones of huge expense and doubtful utility.

There is one further point to be made about sensors. Passive and the conventional type of non-acoustic sensors depend on the opposing submarine's doing something to expose himself– using speed, noisy machinery, periscope or snort. To some extent their effectiveness is within the enemy's control. It is less so with active sonars, even though it can be expected that enemy submarines will use water conditions as effectively as they can. Then there is the question of the technical advances a potential enemy can make to lessen his risk of detection: it seems fair to say that passive sonar is

relatively more sensitive to these than is active sonar.

Another balance to be struck is between crudity and sophistication in anti-submarine weapons. The correct matching of range to the distance at which a fire-control solution is feasible is only one side of the question. There is also the problem of how dead time is to be minimised, and the cost and maintenance penalties of the more sophisticated methods are very important factors to be taken into account when considering alternative solutions – or, to be more precise, the balance of alternative weapon systems; it would be most imprudent of a major anti-submarine maritime force to stake all its kill capability on a single type of weapon untried in war.

Linked to both the sensor and weapon balances is the most cost-critical and controversial of all, the balance between different types of platform. As the next chapter will describe more fully, each has different qualities to offer: the surface ship's long endurance, ability to deploy many diverse systems and command potential; the aircraft's lofted sensors and great tactical mobility; the submarine's innate ability to play the bathymetric game and its logistic autonomy when on patrol. There is a balance to be struck, too, between the sophistication of the platform and of the weapons it carries. You can have, in theory, a simple platform carrying complex weapon systems; you can have a high-quality platform carrying relatively crude weapons; or, very often, the complexity, sophistication and expense

will extend to both platforms and weapons in an attempt to ensure high success rates. It is these last cases that catch the accountant's eye, and the question most commonly asked is where, on the cost-against-effectiveness curve, a particular platform/system arrangement stands. Everyone knows that squeezing out the last 5% of performance may add 50% to the cost: if the system is in that state, however persuasive the operational reasons that got it there, it is vulnerable to the axe.

The striking of these material balances is a process that goes on all the time, and the mix at any given moment will be the product of planning decisions going back 30 years or more. But what it adds up to, when viewed by those who have to operate it, is a list of anti-submarine assets.

Operational Concepts
How these assets are used is determined by operational concepts and tactical thought, and here too balances are to be struck. The most fundamental is that between operations that seek to deny the sea to enemy submarines, and operations that seek to use the sea in spite of enemy submarines.

Sea-denial operations against submarines have not been generally successful in the past. The least successful were offensive patrols by ships, and deep-laid mine barriers; the most successful were Royal Air Force Coastal Command's Bay Offensive, in the mid-1943 phase, and various versions of Operation 'Swamp' from 1944 onwards when immense resources were available. It has been argued, convincingly in my view, that in the conditions of World War 2 assets spent in such operations could often have been more effectively employed in direct support of sea use.

However, the technical conditions have changed. Passive sonar is relatively more sensitive and effective; bottom arrays and sonobuoys are assets of a new kind; the possibility of using submarines as

Left and below:
Three types of anti-submarine platform, all expensive and all with a great deal to offer: the balance between them is one of many that must be struck when planning for anti-submarine warfare.
Crown Copyright

anti-submarine units has greatly increased; command, control and communications are more certain and secure than they were; aircraft have greater endurance. Cumulatively, the result is a great increment in reach. The areas that can be covered by sea-denial forces are quite large, and if the opponent is geographically constricted the potential of sea-denial operations is correspondingly increased.

Sea-denial operations, however, still depend on the opponent's being where he is expected to be, acting in the way he is expected to act and showing the characteristics he is expected to show. Intelligence may correctly predict some of these and operational imperatives may control others; but such expectations have often proved wildly wrong in the past. Moreover, satisfactory attrition rates will always be dependent on things going right: weather, communication and water conditions, enemy non-interference with shore facilities, a correct command and control set-up, and the functioning of equipment in war as well as it did in peace. There have been occasions when wargaming results were based on the assumption that whenever an encounter was theoretically possible, such an encounter would actually happen. This led to a saying, which had some brief vogue, that 'the sky is always blue over West Byfleet'. Assumptions like that are not realistic, and one must beware of them, as one must of heady titles like 'hunter-killer operations', so beloved of the press and so horrifying to old anti-submarine hands, accustomed as they were to looking for needles in haystacks and finding nothing. Sea-denial operations will often, in modern conditions, be more effective than that, but a lot of submarines will always get through.

Sea-use operations will be concerned generally with areas of sea in which ships, whose survival is important to the war, travel. Generally the areas will move; for example, a carrier battle group advancing at a speed of 15kt will carry with it an anti-submarine area of interest that, dependent on the threat, may be as much as 300 miles radius. A convoy may generate a much smaller moving area of interest based on the capabilities of torpedo-firing submarines only. The primary aims of such operations will not be to sink submarines, but sinking submarines will be one of their important functions for two reasons: first, to ensure that the primary aim is unimpaired; second, to inflict the maximum damage on enemy forces.

When the area of interest is very large a great variety of forces may be employed, each as their

Left:
High value units: an area of 300 miles radius round them is of concern, in these days of anti-ship missiles launched from submarines.
Official US Navy photograph

particular attributes best fit them. In the quiet 'deep field' passive sonars are most appropriate and aircraft with their mobility and radar, as well as their ability to deploy sonobuoys, of greatest utility; in the midfield other passive sonars, such as towed arrays, may be brought into play; in the noisy centre, near the high value units, surface ships, helicopters and active sonars will predominate. A large force may have submarines and shore-based fixed-wing aircraft allocated to it, under the control of the seagoing commander. The conduct of such a force, from the broadest elements such as the track it is to follow – critically dependent on water depths and conditions as well as enemy submarine intelligence – to the hour-by-hour stationing of and communicating with a diversity of units above, on and in the sea, is rightly known as integrated anti-submarine warfare and embodies a skill graphically described as water space management.

Such comprehensive measures will not be available for the general protection of shipping, the classical mode of which is the protected convoy. In the days of sailing privateers, the convoy's

accompanying frigates were quick and powerful enough to exact a penalty whose prospect frightened all but the boldest. In both wars, submarines found themselves presented with targets that were concentrated: this meant manoeuvring into an attacking position and, often, breaking radio silence as well. All this increased the detection chances of escorts that were, in any case, concentrated in the right place. Certainly against the submarine, convoy was therefore at least as much an offensive as a defensive device. If the submarines wanted to attack, they had to run the gauntlet. If they chose to hold off, the convoy would achieve its aim of safe and timely arrival.

Nevertheless many commentators, imbued perhaps with offensive spirit or perhaps with notions that there ought to be a better course than just scrummaging one's way through, were always prepared to challenge the concept; and when two new threats arose after 1945, they were quick to pronounce convoy dead. These threats were, first, nuclear attack; and second, the nuclear-powered submarine. The first meant spreading convoys out to anti-nuclear spacing, ships a mile apart. The second meant that a submarine could approach from any angle. Between them, it was said, these developments would put an impossible load on escorts which were of little greater capability, in the crucial field of active sonar, than those of World

Below:
Convoy, the classical method of defending merchant shipping and imposing heavy attrition on submarines. *Imperial War Museum*

War 2. Moreover, aircraft in close support would lack the all-important radar sightings of periscopes and snorts; nuclear submarines would approach, and fire, from deep. It would be impossible to re-route convoys clear of submarine concentrations. Finally, guided missiles could be fired well outside any possible escorting screen.

These are all important factors against the concept of convoy. Yet some of them may be overstated. For example, there is no certainty that nuclear weapons will be an immediate threat. Nor will all the submarines deployed against shipping be nuclear-powered; indeed, according to some authorities the majority will not be. The same goes for guided missile submarines. Finally, whatever the threats, it may for many purposes be necessary to organise merchant shipping into groups: the reasons will vary from the morale effect of grouping under escort to the necessity of controlling the underwater noise pattern.

The objections to convoy led to the idea of protected lanes, a notion whose title was enough to cause apoplexy in many naval officers of my acquaintance. You do not protect water-spaces, you protect ships. Perhaps; but as an alternative to convoy the notion of a lane along which shipping passes, with its flanks protected by prowling anti-submarine forces, has gained some adherents in recent years.

Perhaps the key to its attraction is that active sonar, particularly in ships, has not increased so sharply in range potential as passive sonar has. But passive sonar in a close convoy escort will not work because there is too much noise about. Why not, then, station passive-sonar assets (submarines, towed-array ships, aircraft) on either side of the lane where the noisy merchant ships are and let them take on the submarines making for the lane? This might well be a more cost-effective course than escorted convoys.

The objections to the idea are twofold. First, as with other sea-denial operations, a lot of submarines are bound to get through. And once the wolves are among the sheep, what then? The second is, simply, will merchant seamen agree to sail independently down a lane under threat and without visible escort?

The protected-lane concept is in some ways a more formal way of organising the protection of shipping than convoy, and there are powerful objections to it. It may very well be that elements of both concepts can be combined into a flexible and effective method, and there will be further discussion of this in Chapter 5.

An Integrated Campaign
The operational and tactical balances, then, are at least as important as the material ones. It cannot be stressed too much that they interact. The cycle of the planning process is never-ending, as new threats become apparent, new anti-submarine methods become available, and new people come to the problem with new, and sometimes good, ideas. While planners try with limited resources to cover all the most likely and important eventualities, it will be right for them to remember that the enemy has his problems too, and seek to maximise those problems. The mindless pursuit of the offensive has so far proved disastrous in anti-submarine warfare, but that in no way means that a totally defensive philosophy is called for. To impose the maximum stress, uncertainty and exposure on the opponent is the way to ensure that individual anti-submarine actions, from detection through to kill, are successfully conducted and add up to an integrated, effective anti-submarine campaign.

The Weapons

Platforms and Weapon Systems

One of the more surprising developments in anti-submarine warfare over the past decade has been the way systems designed for one platform have been added to others. Helicopters with dipping sonar have acquired sonobuoys and the associated processing equipment; ships have been fitted with lightweight torpedoes previously, and still, carried by aircraft. Magnetic anomaly detectors go into anything that flies and towed arrays spawn like eels.

If it ever was permissible, therefore, to regard a platform and its associated sensors and weapons as a single, integrated, immutable system, it is no longer sensible to do so. This is not to say that platforms do not have inherent limitations, nor that all are equally effective in carrying the systems they do; it is, however, to say thay their potential for versatility is being pretty well explored.

In the chapter that follows an attempt will be made to deal with each sensor and weapon system under the heading of the platform that is most appropriate to it. This will mean a certain amount of cross-referring for the reader, but if duplication is to be avoided this is inevitable.

The Shore

Shore facilities have an important part to play in large scale anti-submarine warfare. They are far less power-and space-limited than anything afloat or in the air, and therefore can provide enormous data storage and handling capacity and very powerful communications transmitters, including some unique systems such as very low frequency communication with submerged submarines. Communications satellites, which can only be put into orbit by shore launchers, give the opportunity of passing to forces at sea a very large amount of data.

This potential is particularly apparent in the United States' arrangements for the processing and transmission of SOSUS data, as reported in the technical press. Under the sponsorship of the Defence Advance Research Project Agency (DARPA), the SOSUS system is now in its fifth or sixth generation. The responses from this network of bottom-mounted passive arrays are fed, after several stages of initial refinement, into an extremely powerful shore-side computer called ILLIAC-4, evaluated and passed to all the authorities, both ashore and at sea, who need to know. The need for complex evaluation machinery is, of course, driven by the complexity and often tenuous nature of the SOSUS indications themselves; and in war, when some SOSUS installations might be lost through enemy action and the remainder supplemented by air-laid Rapidly Deployable Sonar Systems (RDSS) and surveillance towed arrays deployed from civilian-manned ships (TAGOS), new complexities would be introduced.

Shore headquarters handle the allocation and tasking of maritime anti-submarine forces in the broadest sense. In particular, the missions and assignment of shore-based aircraft will be matters for decision by the authorities ashore, as will the operation of some submarines. Just how much autonomy is given to the seagoing commanders, and what shore-based aircraft and submarines are to come under their control, are matters to be decided by the operational headquarters ashore; of the lessons learnt in peacetime exercises, this will be one of the most important.

Finally, one use of shore facilities, envisaged apparently by the Soviet Union, should be kept in mind. This is the employment of shore-based nuclear-headed missiles to attack submarine probability areas. It is clearly a measure to be used against ballistic missile submarines in the event of a decision to carry out a first strike: crude but, unfortunately, not quite incredible.

Surface Ships

Surface ships have many functions other than anti-submarine warfare, and their vulnerabilities as well as their potencies are as much above the surface as beneath it. When discussing the anti-submarine function it is necessary to keep in the back of one's mind their other preoccupations.

The most unique and arguably the most important function of surface ships in anti-submarine warfare is the command and control of forces at sea. Straddling the interface as they do, equipped with a comprehensive range of communication equipments as they are, full of data processing and display equipment as they can be, they are in the best state to have a full grasp of the situation. This applies particularly to the operations of protected groups, whether combatant or trade shipping; barrier operations may be better conducted from the shore.

The equipments carried by a large surface ship suitable for a force commander are too numerous to mention individually. They will certainly include satellite communications to and from the shore and other major units equipped and in a position to hear them. Data rates on these communication links are constantly improving and, in the US Navy in particular, computers ashore will be able to feed shipborne computers, ensuring a picture in the force

commander's ship that shows all the available data. Its value is, as sceptics will be quick to point out, directly related to the quality of the data. Garbage in, garbage out; and large amounts of information on the same set of targets can, if they do not match, cause foul-ups of undreamed-of dimensions. But sensible interpretation in such circumstances is what staffs and commands are paid for.

The large surface ship does in any case have from its own sensors a great deal of information. Air warning radar, supplemented in many cases by airborne early warning from organic aircraft, provides a picture of the air situation, enemy and friendly, for up to 250 miles around. Airborne early warning is also an excellent check on friendly surface units over the radar horizon. Above-water communications, both satellite and direct, with other ships and aircraft in the force will enable the commander to extend his view of the situation. Communication with submarines is more difficult. It is not that the means do not exist. Submarines can break surface to communicate by radio; or they can come to a depth where a trailing wire aerial will establish radio communication; or they can release a transmitting buoy such as the American AN/BRT-1, which repeats a pre-recorded message; or they can communicate by underwater telephone with a

Normally the command and control function is combined, in a large surface combatant, with the ability to carry numerous other anti-submarine assets. Typically these are helicopters; sometimes also fixed-wing aircraft as in the American, French and some South American navies; and sometimes relatively long-range anti-submarine missiles as in the latest Soviet cruisers. These systems will all be discussed in later sections.

So far no navy has taken the step of separating the two big-ship functions – command and control on the one hand, and garaging and operating anti-submarine aircraft on the other. But the idea has been mooted often enough, most seriously in the United States 'Arapaho' concept which has been in being for at least 10 years and was tested at sea in October 1982. In this system a container merchant ship is specially fitted out with preplanned and prefabricated aircraft operating facilities and operates a small squadron of helicopters in a variety of roles, the most usual being convoy escort, support for underway replenishment groups, and support for amphibious landings. It is not doubted that Arapaho can work in practical terms. The only quesion is whether it is a sensible use of resources; after all, the basic concept of such ships as the 'Invincible' class accepted that it was more cost-effective to combine helicopter-carrying and command facilities in one ship rather than separate them in two. And in the United States Navy, the inbuilt tendency to favour the strike role, rather than the anti-submarine, militates against diversion of resources to Arapaho. Nevertheless if a need is seen to get more anti-submarine helicopters to sea than present platforms can manage, Arapaho is the best answer for that quick augmentation; and the facts that blueprints exist, and that the Royal Navy has converted the container ship *Astronomer* (now renamed *Reliant*) for a similar role, are to be welcomed.

Smaller surface ships – frigates and destroyers – are at the sharper end of anti-submarine warfare. In

Above:
An early Soviet essay in large ASW ships: the helicopter carrier *Leningrad*. *Crown Copyright*

Below:
The second generation, no longer classified solely as an ASW vessel by the Soviet Navy: *Minsk* with a British squadron in attendance. *Crown Copyright*

link ship. The problem is that none of these methods is renowned for first-time reliability, and all are tactically limiting to the submarine; particularly if in contact with the enemy, he may be extremely reluctant to use them. Time spent away from optimum depth in order to establish communication is time lost.

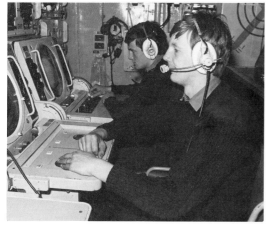

World War 2, ships sank more submarines than any other type of anti-submarine unit, though shore-based aircraft ran them very close. It is to be doubted whether they would produce the same record in any future large-scale conflict (though if their medium and light helicopters were regarded as organic parts of the ship weapon system, they might score surprisingly high), but statistics are not really the point. What is more important is the contribution they make to the whole anti-submarine battle, and that includes their deterrent effect on the enemy, the comfort they can give to friends, the co-ordination they can effect between disparate units, and the point of application of their particular talents.

For most surface ships that point of application is still close to the force or convoy centre, in a noisy environment where sonic precision is necessary. This is best provided by active sonar and that, of course, is what most surface ships still have. The most advanced active sets are of high power and low frequency, their transducers mounted in bow domes that project like chins under water. Such sonars are the American AN/SQS-26 and AN/SQS-53, which, it is claimed, not only reach out to the first convergence zone in favourable conditions but employ the so-called bottom-bounce mode to give long detection ranges. Type 2016, the latest British hull-mounted sonar, appears to adopt a rather different philosophy and to emphasise reliability of detection and classification. Digital data processing allows the operator to make a very close examination of target structure. France and Canada produce hull-mounted sonars but both nations have continued to fit variable-depth sonars, the idea of which – to lower the sonar to the optimum operating depth and therby gain sonic advantage – is fine but the practicalities, in a frigate-sized ship, dubious. All modern active sonar sets have panoramic presentation, that is to say they make simultaneous

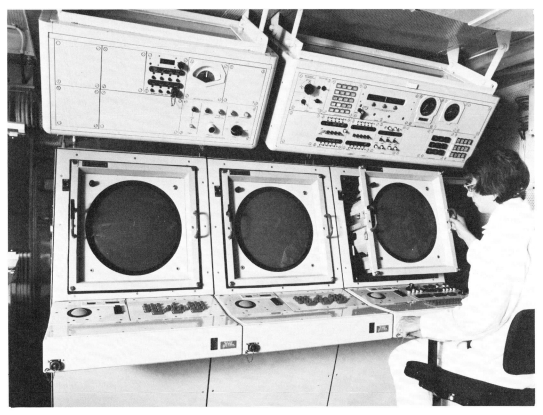

transmissions along an all-round set of beams which are 'pre-formed' by the configuration of the transducer and the mode of transmission. In this way one avoids the time lags that were caused by stepping the beam five degrees at a time in the old-style 'searchlight' sonars.

Lightweight sonars for use in small vessels are not neglected by European manufacturers. In the Netherlands, for example, Hollandse Signaal Apparaten produce the PHS-32 and PHS-36, which employ all the techniques that have already been described but are naturally of much lower power and by definition have to operate from a bouncier platform. Plessey in the United Kingdom make the PMS-26 and 27, which derive from their parent – a dunking helicopter sonar – a particularly good classification facility based on doppler.

Weapons associated with active sonars must clearly be designed to match the maximum ranges such sonars achieve. As has already been observed, the laws of physics and the anomalies of the sea's structure will ensure that there is no simple answer to the question 'What is the maximum range?' But for modern high-power sonars, ranges in the duct can be of the order 10 miles though they are often less; while convergence zone ranges are about 30 or, in the rarer cases where the second convergence zone yields a contact, 60 miles. There is thus something of a dilemma: should all shipborne anti-submarine weapons reach out to the second convergence zone, and thereby lose accuracy close in, or should there be a variety of them to cover the various ranges?

In fact, the evolutionary history of anti-submarine weapons has ensured that plenty of variety exists. The most basic and shortest-range of all, the depth charge, still exists as the most widely-fitted single weapon; one notices it peeping shyly out of the columns of *Jane's Fighting Ships* in no less than 30 navies. Anti-submarine mortars, throwing bombs a distance of a few thousand yards, are almost as common; the British Limbo (Mortar Mark 10) is in many navies, as are the Swedish 375mm launcher and a French model. The Russians and their clients have a whole family of rocket launchers (Raketnaya Bombometnaya Ustanovka, or RBU) whose range, at the widest reported span, is 1,400 to 6,400 yd. Whether, like other thrown weapons, they are fuzed to burst at a certain depth or, like the old Hedgehog, on impact with a solid object, is uncertain; but it is more likely to be the former. And they throw up to 16 at a time.

It is customary to despise these relatively crude and short-range weapons. The assumption seems to be that no self-respecting submarine would allow itself to get within range of them and that in any case a nuclear could outstrip their sinking-time by using speed, depth and manoeuvre. All this may hold good in some cases, but in such a situation there are almost bound to be many units about; it will not be all that simple for a submarine to sort out where they are, and, particularly, how far away. And of course not all submarines are nuclear-powered. Nor should surface ships be too ashamed if an opportunity for attack with such weapons occurs only after a torpedoing and consequent alerting of surface escorts. Counter-attacks of that sort occurred very frequently in World War 2 and must have accounted for a high proportion of U-boats sunk.

More and more surface ships are also being fitted with tube launching systems for lightweight torpedoes. Given a sonar contact classified submarine, and a certain amount of tracking, a ship can launch a torpedo towards a computed future position where the torpedo can start its self-homing operations. The speed of the torpedo on its 'fore-run' to this position, and whether it alerts the target submarine in time for the latter to take effective avoiding action, are critical factors for success. Again, the opportunities for counter-attack should not be discounted; indeed it has been suggested that the prospect of having a torpedo fired back at it, down the bearing of the hydrophone effect from its own torpedoes, might put a submarine off from attacking in the first place.

Clearly, however, delivery ranges beyond the narrow scope of ship-launched or ship-dropped weapons are needed to match the limits of the active-sonar envelope and to give the opportunity of firing on data provided by other units. Nearly all the measures in this category demand the distant delivery of a self-homing torpedo.

Below:
The Swedish Bofors 375mm anti-submarine rocket launcher. *Bofors Ordnance AB*

Bottom:
The Belgian frigate *Westdiep*. A French six-barrelled rocket launcher is abaft the gun. *Rolls-Royce photograph*

One way of getting the torpedo to a target area is by rocket. Three systems are available in the West. The most widely fitted is the American ASROC (an acronym too obvious to need explanation) which carries a Mark 44 or Mark 46 lightweight torpedo. It has a ballistic trajectory and its range is between about 1.25nm (2km) and 10nm (16km). A dozen navies, including six in NATO, fit this weapon. A common anti-submarine weapon (CASW) is under development in the USA and will eventually replace ASROC. Britain and Australia jointly developed the Ikara: this is a winged missile with a range of about 10nm (16km) which is command-guided to the target area, monitored by a specialised control radar. At the computed dropping point, the missile is commanded to release its torpedo, which parachutes into the water. Again, the Mark 44 or Mark 46 torpedo can be used. The French have a ramp-launched system called Malafon, the most like a pilotless aircraft of the three. Like Ikara it has midcourse guidance but the main flight is unpowered. The torpedo it carries is

Table 5: Surface Ship AS Weapons

Number in service	Number of navies	Country of origin	Designation	Type	Range (yd)	Number of projectiles	Remarks
1,000+	30+	Var	–	Depth Charge	Nil	Up to 5	Includes throwers out to 200 yd
166	20	USA	Hedgehog	Spigot Mortar	350	24	Contact fuze
8	1	Italy	Lanciabas	Mortar	1,000	3	ISD 1956
47	1	USSR	RBU-1000	Rocket	1,200	6	ISD 1962 (2)
194	12	USSR	RBU-1200	Rocket	1,400	5	ISD 1956 (2)
15	1	France	–	Rocket	1,600	6	ISD 1964/73
57	8	UK	Mark 10 (Limbo)	Mortar	2,000	3	ISD 1955
14	2	France	–	Mortar	2,700	4	ISD 1959
126	2	USSR	RBU-2500	Rocket	2,800	16	ISD 1955
7	1	Norway	Terne	Rocket	3,000	6	ISD 1961
70	15	Sweden	Bofors	Rocket	3,600	4	ISD 1957
260	8	USSR	RBU-6000	Rocket	6,400	12	ISD 1960
265	12	USA	ASROC	Rocket Torpedo Carrier	12,000	8	Lightweight torpedoes carried
12	1	France	Malafon	Rocket Torpedo Carrier	16,000	1	L4 torpedo carried
19	3	UK/Aus	Ikara	Rocket Torpedo Carrier	20,000	1	Lightweight Torpedo carried
2	1	USSR	FRAS-1	Nuclear	30,000	2	ISD 1968
55	1	USSR	SS-N-14	Rocket Torpedo Carrier	60,000	2-4	ISD 1968

(ISD: In Service Date)

Notes
1. Many nations fit tubes for ship-launched lightweight torpedoes; see page 86 for torpedo characteristics. Well over 200 systems are in use worldwide, mostly on major war vessels of modern construction
2. Many RBU systems are 'doubled', giving twice the number of projectiles shown per ship.

the French L4, a relatively heavy weapon, and the range is reported to be 8nm (13km). In the Soviet Union a similar system has existed since 1970. At first thought to be a short-range surface-to-surface weapon, it is now as the SS-N-14 firmly classified as being ASW in nature. It is carried in the 'Kara' and 'Kresta II' cruisers and 'Krivak' frigates.

All these weapon systems have short times of flight and so can put a torpedo in the water quickly. This is a considerable tactical advantage since a submarine, once localised and tracked long enough for a fire control solution to be achieved, can be attacked almost at once. No doubt by then he will be alerted and taking avoiding action, but at least the dangers of losing contact are minimised. The systems also have the advantage of 24-hour availability and all-weather performance.

The other main method of distant delivery of anti-submarine weapons, the small or medium helicopter, is likely to be more limited by weather and darkness or poor visibility, and to have a slower speed of reaction. Pilots cannot be sitting strapped in 24 hours a day on the offchance that a submarine will be contacted. On the other hand, the helicopter offers more flexibility. Not only does it have a longer range than the rocket systems, but it is

Top:
Firing of an anti-submarine torpedo from a ship-mounted tube. *Crown Copyright*

Above:
British ship-launched torpedo weapon system tubes (STWS) under construction. *The Plessey Co Ltd*

Below left:
A 'Brooke' class frigate of the US Navy. The ASROC launcher is forward of the bridge. *US Navy Official photograph*

Below:
Launch of an Ikara missile. *Crown Copyright*

conducted by a sentient human being who can adapt to last-minute changes of the situation. The most common method of torpedo delivery from a helicopter of this kind is still probably the vectored attack, where a directing unit–either the ship, or an aircraft, in firm contact with the target–computes a dropping point and, monitoring the helicopter on its radar, instructs it to fly the necessary courses and to drop its weapon load.

But small-ship helicopters have other potential versatilities in the ASW field. Many are now being fitted with their own sonic systems. For example, the Westland-Sud Aviation Lynx has in the version supplied to the German Navy a Bendix DAQS-18 dipping sonar, particularly suitable for the North Sea operations for which the parent ships were designed. This was a privately-funded develop-ment, as is Plessey's HISOS-1 lightweight dipping

sonar, which uses a physically extending, wide-bandwidth transducer array giving long range and good bearing accuracy. Sonobuoy systems could also be used. The Lynx could no doubt carry an outfit of buoys and the necessary processing equipment: the Marconi Lightweight Acoustic Processing and Display System (LAPADS AQS-902) is already available, and can moreover accept HISOS-1 data, though it would probably need a considerably uprated Lynx to take the extra weight of both dipping sonar and sonobuoy outfits. But the most ambitious development by far in the business of sonobuoy deployment from small-ship helicopters has been the American LAMPS-III system, and this deserves a paragraph to itself.

LAMPS stands for Light Airborne Multi-Purpose System, which goes some way towards describing a radical concept: namely, the airborne extension of

Left:
The Australian frigate *Yarra* and the British *Leander*, showing alternative positions for Ikara. *Yarra's* is right aft, allowing retention of the 4.5in gun turret.
Crown Copyright

Above:
The Soviet anti-submarine cruiser *Udaloy,* which can carry two helicopters.   *Crown Copyright*

the ship's sensor and weapon reach. The helicopter is really a relay station, a manoeuvrable platform that drops sensors at command (even the button is pressed in the ship and not the aircraft), picks up the raw data on its sonobuoy receivers and sends it straight back to the ship via the ubiquitous data link for processing, and manoeuvres to a dropping position to release torpedoes on command. The aircraft does in fact have a crew of three, and enough systems to enable it to operate autonomously if need be, but in theory it is the ship that calls the shots because it is in possession of all the available information and the helicopter's knowledge is only partial. Nevertheless the helicopter, the SH-60B, is a heavy machine with an operating weight of 21,780lb (9,900kg), more than twice that of the Lynx, and needs elaborate handling arrangements including wire hauldowns, automatic traps and a railway to move it into its hangar from the flight deck.

The LAMPS programme has gone through a good many troubles, and the LAMPS—I system with its helicopter the SH-2F is reported to have been severely weather-limited and by no means an unqualified success, although it will continue in older ships until the late 1990s. The US Navy's persistence is shown by its order for over 200 LAMPS-III helicopters to operate from four newer classes of ship, the CG-47 guided missile cruisers, DD-963 and DD-993 destroyers and FFG-7 Block 3 frigates. There is one fact about these ship classes that is, perhaps, the key to the US Navy's conviction that it needs LAMPS: they are all to be fitted with towed passive sonar arrays.

The passive sonar towed array may well be the most important single development in shipboard ASW sensors since 1945. In a sense, of course, it is not new at all: the Nash Fish of 1917 was indeed a towed hydrophone array. No doubt that had one of the merits of the present system, the ability to lie in quiet water well away from the noises attendant on the ship's passage. What it did not have was the current array's great range of frequency, nor its ability to ride at depths where the effects of temperature gradients are minimised, nor the highly sophisticated signal processing equipment on board the ship.

The towed array on which most information has been released is the AN/SQR-19 TACTAS, produced by Gould Defense Electronics and General Electric Company in America. The towed body consists essentially of eight acoustic modules containing hydrophones and electronics; a further module which senses depth, temperature and heading; and a telemetry drive module which transmits data to the ship via an armoured towing cable which incorporates a coaxial conductor. The towing cable measures 5,600ft (1,713m) which gives some idea of the depth-flexibility of the equipment. It is claimed that TACTAS can be effectively employed at high speeds, but a NATO report only two years ago suggests the optimum towing speed at 8-12kt. Even if the lower figure were taken, sprint-and-drift techniques could be employed to give much useful listening time, though clearly slow towing speeds would be some limitation.

It is clear from the literature that the equipment produces the sort of information available from most advanced passive sonar systems: that is to say

indications of submarine noise both broad and narrow band across a wide range of frequencies, with spectral-line displays to aid classification, and indication of bearing. Ranges can be expected to be generally long, and it is significant that one of the advantages claimed for the LAMPS-III system is that it can operate out to the third convergence zone. For, of course, TACTAS on its own can only complete the first two stages of the anti-submarine process, detection and classification. Localisation must be achieved by another unit or system, and no doubt it is hoped that the LAMPS-III helicopter, operating from the detecting ship and acting really as an extension of it, will be able to complete the job. If another unit needs to be called in, the command, control and communications organisation of the force must be able to handle it.

Both British and French navies are entering the towed-array field. So far as the Royal Navy is concerned, this appears to be whole-hearted and limited only by funds. Fitting is more likely to be in new construction though there is a limited retrospective programme, and indeed at one time the new Type 23 frigate was being canvassed as a simple towed-array ship. France may move more slowly, though she plans to install in some new ships a towed array called Flûte; she has a good deal staked in variable-depth active sonars and more of her fleet is deployed in the Mediterranean where waters of depth suitable for towed-array work, although extensive, are not quite the same as the broad reaches of the Atlantic. It can also be predicted that neither navy will adopt the LAMPS-III concept: they will accept neither its technical complexities nor its very large helicopters, and will prefer to rely on more autonomously operated aircraft with highly-trained crews.

As for the Soviet Navy, there is no firm evidence yet of surface-ship towed arrays and helicopters may not yet have gone seriously into the sonobuoy

business; even the new Helix, carried in the 'Udaloy' class ASW cruisers, appears to be essentially an active 'dunker'.

Aircraft ASW Systems: Rotary Wing

So far we have discussed helicopters that can be regarded essentially as extensions of their parent ships' ASW capability. It is now time to look at helicopters that are ASW assets in their own right, limited only – as are all heavier-than-air aircraft – by fuel and crew fatigue considerations that entail their returning to their ship or shore base after a few hours' sortie.

The unique characteristic of the helicopter is that it can hover above the surface. This means that, invulnerable to current submarine weapon systems, a helicopter of suitable size and power can put an active sonar transducer into still water, at the desired depth if the amount of cable carried allows. It can carry enough processing and display

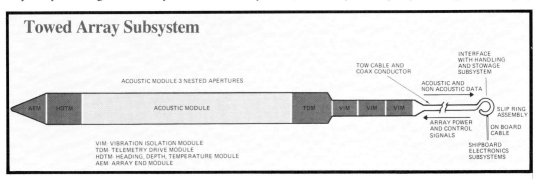

Towed Array Subsystem

ACOUSTIC MODULE 3 NESTED APERTURES

TOW CABLE AND COAX CONDUCTOR

INTERFACE WITH HANDLING AND STOWAGE SUBSYSTEM

ACOUSTIC AND NON ACOUSTIC DATA

AEM HDTM | ACOUSTIC MODULE | TDM | VIM | VIM | VIM

SLIP RING ASSEMBLY

ARRAY POWER AND CONTROL SIGNALS

ON BOARD CABLE

SHIPBOARD ELECTRONICS SUBSYSTEMS

VIM: VIBRATION ISOLATION MODULE
TDM: TELEMETRY DRIVE MODULE
HDTM: HEADING, DEPTH, TEMPERATURE MODULE
AEM: ARRAY END MODULE

equipment to enable its crew to classify, localise and track contacts, and weapons to attempt destruction of a submarine once a fire control solution has been obtained.

The large helicopter can thus be presented as a comprehensive anti-submarine search and attack system, capable at all stages of the ASW process, and not suffering two of the principal drawbacks of the surface ship as an active sonar platform: that is to say the noise surrounding the transducer and the shallow depth at which it must operate. The helicopter is therefore theoretically a better sonar platform. However, it is impossible to provide in a helicopter the level of electrical supply needed to drive a high-powered, low-frequency active sonar, nor could it possibly lift the equipments associated with such sets.

Consequently the dunking-sonar helicopter's reach at any given time will be measured in thousands, rather than tens of thousands, of yards although its certainty of detection and classification may well be superior to those of ship-mounted sonars in many conditions, and its mobility and

Left:
The US Navy's SH-3 helicopter, the Sikorsky original from which European variants were derived
US Navy Official photograph

Above:
The latest version of the Sea King, the Mark 5, which often uses sonobuoys as its primary sensor.
Crown Copyright

unpredictability of movement will be a constant worry to any submarine that can hear its transmissions or knows in any other way that it is about. These factors add up to a clear role for the dunking-sonar helicopter as both a screening and pouncing vehicle at distances of up to say 15 miles from the high-value targets in a combatant force, or from the fringes of a convoy.

This is useful but does not necessarily satisfy the force commander who is concerned about the threat from guided missile submarines, particularly those like the 'Charlie' class that can fire from submerged positions on their own sonar information from ranges of 30 miles or so. Consequently, some 10 years ago advantage was taken of improvements in sonobuoys and processing equipment to give heavy helicopters a passive capability that would increase their scope and, to a degree, change the pattern of their operations.

The changes have not been uniform throughout the navies of the West. The United States, for reasons that will become apparent later in this chapter, has not gone very far in its modification to its main heavy helicopter, the SH-3. Its chief sensor is still the AN/AQS-13 active sonar operating in the 10KHz band, a set which is a well-evolved improvement on a distinguished original, much trusted by its users and proven in a rigorous series of trials and exercises. The machine does carry a limited outfit of sonobuoys and a processor, but these are adjuncts rather than a primary system and the helicopter's main role is seen as screening and pouncing in the inner zone. It can of course carry lightweight torpedoes, or depth charges including nuclear ones. The main problem with these aircraft is that they are ageing and need replacement. No

Above:
Sea King Mk 5 dropping a torpedo.
Crown Copyright

Right:
LAPADS installation in a Sea King Mk 5.
Marconi Avionics Limited

decision appears yet to have been taken on a successor, but a dunking-sonar version of the SH-60, designated the SH-60F, has been identified as a logical solution.

The Royal Navy has gone much further into the passive sonobuoy role and the deep field. Its Sea King helicopters, confined in the Mark 1 and Mark 2 versions to Type 195 or dunking sonars, have

Table 6: Rotary Wing AS Aircraft

Type	Country of origin	Length rotors turning	Rotor diam	Max speed	Engines	Max take-off weight	Endurance	Remarks
Super Frelon SA321G	France	75ft 6in (23.03m)	62ft 0in (18. 9m)	148kt	3×1,170Kw Turbomeca Turmo IIC	28,660lb (13,000kg)	4hr	ISD 1966. Operates from *Jeanne D'Arc*. Can also operate from carriers or shore
Super Puma AS332F	France	61ft 5in (18.73m)	51ft 2in (15.58m)	160kt	2×1,327Kw Turbomeca Makila Ia	19,180lb (8,700kg)	3hr 20min	Two torpedoes and sonar or MAD and sonobuoys
Agusta Bell 212 ASW	Italy	57ft 1in (17.40m)	48ft 0in (14.63m)	110kt	1×1,398Kw Pratt & Whitney PT6T-6	11,200lb (5,080kg)	3hr 12min	Under licence from Bell. Dipping sonar. 2 torpedoes or 2 DCs. Operated also by Greek and Spanish navies
Agusta Sikorsky SH-3D/H	Italy	72ft 8in (22.15m)	62ft 0in (18.90m)	144kt	2×1,118Kw GE T-58 G-100	21,000lb (9,525kg)	4hr 30 min	LF dipping sonar. 4 torpedoes or DCs. Operated also by several South American navies.
Ka-25 ('Hormone')	USSR	51ft 8in (15.74m)	51ft 8in (15.74m)	113kt	2×671Kw Grushenkov GTD-3	20,900lb (9,500kg)	2hr	Dipping sonar, towed MAD, torpedoes and DCs.
Ka-32 ('Helix')	USSR	55ft 0in (16.75m)	55ft 0in (16.75m)	–	–	–	–	Outfit probably includes sonobuoys
Westland Sea King HAS Mk 5	UK	72ft 8in (22.15m)	62ft 0in (18.90m)	144kt	2×1,238Kw Rolls Royce Gnome H-1400-1	21,000lb (9,525kg)	4hr 30min	Originally under licence from Sikorsky. 4 torpedoes or DCs. Earlier versions operated by Australia, Norway India, Egypt, Belgium. Mk 5 has extensive sonobuoy fit.
Westland Lynx HAS MK 2	UK/ France	49ft 9in (15.16m)	42ft 0in (12.80m)	125kt	2×559Kw Rolls-Royce Gem 2	10,500lb (4,763kg)	2hr	With Sud Aviation (France). Engines uprated in later versions, 2 torpedoes. Dipping sonar can be fitted. Operated by 10 countries
Sikorsky SH-3H	USA	72ft 8in (22.15m)	62ft 0in (18.90m)	144kt	2×1,044Kw GE T-58 GE-10	21,000lb (9,525kg)	4hr	Dipping sonar. Small sonobuoy outfit.
Sikorsky SH-60B	USA	64ft 10in (19.76m)	53ft 8in (16.36m)	126kt	2×1,260Kw GE T-700 GE-401	21,780lb (9,900kg)	2hr 18min	LAMPS-III. 25-tube launcher for sonobuoys. Torpedoes or DCs.

acquired in the Mark 5 a large sonobuoy outfit and a LAPADS processor which can display 'hard copy' responses from four sonobuoys at once. The aircrew – two pilots, a so called observer (surely the least appropriate title for an officer in any maritime force) as tactical director, and an aircrewman to handle the sensors – are well-practised in sonobuoy tracking as in all other tactics, and reckon only to use active sonar in the final stages of an attack. Confirmation of the presence of a submarine can be obtained from MAD equipment which, unlike most helicopter MADs which are flown as external 'birds', is integrated into the aircraft structure.

Sea King helicopters have, of course, been exported to many other countries and in many versions. In general, those supplied in the ASW role are still active-sonar vehicles. This raises, or at least sharpens, the question of what will happen when Sea King replacements are required. The Westland and Agusta Companies of Britain and Italy respectively have formed a joint company called EH Industries to manage a collaborative programme for a helicopter to be called the EH101. The specification for this aircraft includes dunking and sonobuoy systems with appropriate processing, so it appears that a wide range of ASW roles will be available: an attractive prospect when combined with a five-hour endurance. It will perhaps be a pity if the United States cannot wait for the appearance of this aircraft, the prototype of which is due to fly in 1986, to replace its HS-3s; a large US contract would make more of a reality of the 'two-way street' in defense procurement, of which so much has been heard and so little seen.

France has not entered the large ASW helicopter field so comprehensively as the UK. There is a steady history of dunking sonars produced by Sintra-Alcatel, and the latest, the HS-12, has many attractive features including relatively light weight and a claimed ability to determine essential target data after only two transmissions. Heavy helicopters are the super Frelon and possibly later the Super Puma, and French Lynxes are fitted with active sonar. Sonobuoy data processing systems are available in various versions. But the main impression from the literature is of a somewhat unsystematic programme for the French Navy, with equipment plans driven as much by export prospects as by operational requirements.

Soviet helicopter ASW has so far rested with the Kamov Ka-25, code-named 'Hormone', though a major development called 'Helix' is now in service. The 'Hormone A', the· ASW version, is a large 20,900lb (9,500kg) helicopter with, apparently, dipping sonar as its main sensor. There is no information on whether it or the Helix employ sonobuoys extensively. If, as some Western commentators suggest, the Soviet ASW effort of the 1970s was directed against ballistic missile submarines, this concentration of systems of relatively short reach is surprising. It might be explainable on the assumption that the Russians wanted to get something to sea quickly, but one would have expected that by now they would have come up with systems more appropriate to the role – if that is the role. On the other hand, these very orthodox helicopters may be provided for a very orthodox task: screen-and-pounce for an all-purpose combatant force. There is no shortage of them; the 'Kiev' class can carry 22, the 'Moskva' class 18.

Aircraft ASW Systems: Fixed Wing
Five navies – those of Argentina, Brazil, France, India and the United States – operate fixed-wing anti-submarine aircraft from aircraft carriers. Most of them are developments or derivations of a Grumman design of the 1950s; in those days the main sensor was radar and the aircraft were

deployed against conventional submarines which had to expose snort masts above the surface. Some sonobuoys were carried to maintain contact once the submarine had dived but the kill stood to be delivered by helicopter or surface craft detached from the main force.

This is probably the principle on which the S-2 variants of the Argentine and Brazilian navies and the Alizés of the French and Indian navies still operate. While it is fair to say that budgetary considerations have more to do with this limitation of capability than any operational assessment, it is nevertheless true that conventional submarines are seen as a threat to all these navies in many circumstances and the aircraft are therefore useful.

The United States Navy, however, has gone into another generation of aircraft and with it another concept, more suited to a threat from nuclear-powered submarines. The Lockheed S-3 Viking is a jet aircraft of which the full potential is still being explored. Its chief sensor is undoubtedly the sonobuoy, of which it carries an impressive stock, but it also has a radar which is much relied upon by its operators since it has an excellent performance against both snort masts and periscopes. Data from both these sources is fed into a modern and high-capacity processor which can also receive, via a data link, information from external sources. The presence in the aircraft of a Tactical Control Officer (TACCO), specially skilled in the co-ordination, handling and exploitation of such data, is another asset.

The S-3 is a great help to any force commander because it can operate in one of his zones of greatest preoccupation, that is the area between two and three hundred miles from the force centre where submarines of the 'Echo', 'Juliet' and 'Oscar' classes could be an immediate threat. Whether the aircraft carries out a mainly radar patrol, on the lookout for submarines rising to a firing position; or monitors a sonobuoy field sown by itself; or co-operates with towed array units operating in the deep field, will depend on the tactical situation. Whatever it does, it

Table 7: Fixed Wing AS Aircraft: Ship-Based

Type	Country of origin	Length	Wingspan	Speed	Max take-off weight	Engines	Endurance	Remarks
Alizé	France	45ft 6in (13.66m)	51ft 2in (15.60m)	254kt	18,100lb (8,217kg)	1×Rolls-Royce Dart MK 21	3hr 45min	ISD 1960. Modernisation in progress: improved radar and navigation. Also operated by Indian Navy.
Tracker S-2	USA	43ft 6in (13.26m)	72ft 7in (22.13m)	280kt	24,500lb (11,123kg)	2×Wright R-1820-82A	5hr	ISD 1954. Still operated by several South American navies.
Viking S-3	USA	53ft 4in (16.26m)	68ft 8in (20.93m)	500kt	42,500lb (19,295kg)	2×GE TF-34 GE-2	5hr	ISD 1975. Sonobuoy, processor and MK 46 torpedo fit.

will be a considerable problem for any submarine commander – whether he knows it is there or not.

The Royal Navy, of course, no longer has ships that can carry fixed wing anti-submarine aircraft. In fact the ASW Gannet, the last such aircraft in the Fleet Air Arm, was phased out well before the last of the carriers that could operate it, probably because the airborne early warning (AEW) version was considered a more operationally important way of employing the remaining airframes. As was shown in the Falklands campaign, organic air resources are always precious in distant waters, but it is probably right to regard the AEW function as the more vital; after all, the Sea King Mark 5 does provide a sophisticated organic passive-sonar capability, and fixed-wing ASW effort can be provided in many geographical areas by shorebased aircraft. It is to these that we now turn.

Shore-based ASW aircraft have a long and distinguished history. By the end of World War 1 over 650 aircraft were employed in this duty; the fact that many were seaplanes and airships does not invalidate the principle. They were much feared by the U-boats, who often refrained from attacking convoys with an air escort. In World War 2 RAF Coastal Command, starting with inadequate resources, built up to a formidable strength with aircraft of very long range, good radar and adequate weapons. They were flown by crews of high skill and spirit in offensive roles – particularly in the Bay Offensive – and also in support of convoys, and were very effective in both. On the other side of the Atlantic, the US Navy's shore-based aircraft and airships scored many successes of their own. Once again, submarines were often inhibited from moving into attacking positions by the presence of aircraft.

Below:
The Anglo-Italian EH-101 helicopter, entering service in the 1990s. *EH Industries Ltd*

After World War 2 the new dimension given to conventional submarine operations by the invention of the snort mast sharpened the requirement for aircraft to be able to detect and attack boats transiting submerged to their patrol areas. This was met by the introduction of better radars and submerged tracking by sonobuoys once a submarine had dived, which it generally did once its search receivers indicated that it had been detected.

But a much greater challenge to the long range maritime patrol (LRMP) aircraft was developing with the introduction of the nuclear-powered submarine. Against it, radar was no use unless the submarine for tactical reasons put something above the surface. This was not likely to happen unless the submarine was about to carry out an attack, when the aircraft might be too late to take preventive action, or was unwary, which seemed to happen rather often with the Russians in peace but was less likely in war. Aircraft might still be some deterrent to submarines seeking attacking positions, and

would of course still be effective against conventionals, but this would scarcely justify their expense.

The situation was changed by several factors, all connected with underwater noise and its detection by passive means. First, Soviet submarines were satisfactorily noisy. Second, the SOSUS system gave a wide-area indication of submarine presence. Third, better quality and supplies of sonobuoys and processing equipment gave long range maritime patrol aircraft a means of localising and tracking submarines detected by SOSUS or by other means. Fourth, lightweight torpedoes improved the possibility of such aircraft carrying the ASW process through to a kill.

Right:
The Ka-25 'Hormone', standard helicopter of the Soviet Navy. *Crown Copyright*

Below:
The French carrier *Clemenceau* with Alizé aircraft ranged port side aft and Super-Frelon helicopters amidships. *French Navy Official photograph*

Above:
Viking S-3 aircraft of the US Navy.
US Navy Official Photograph

Together, and matched with aircraft whose endurance was moving into the 10hr plus category, these improvements maintained a viable anti-submarine role for the long range maritime patrol aircraft. At least three distinct tasks can be visualised for it. First, it can be used as an anti-submarine probe: acting on SOSUS or other indications of submarine probability, it can search the area with sonobuoys and, once in contact and tracking, can carry out an attack with its own weapons. Second, it can carry out independent area operations, monitoring its patrol area either by radar or by overflying a sonobuoy barrier it, or its predecessor, has laid. Finally, it can operate very much as the S-3 Viking generally does, in direct support in the deep or mid-field round a protected force. In all these modes it has the opportunity to co-operate with other ASW forces.

The most widely-distributed, as well as the most heavily-promoted, modern LRMP aircraft is the Lockheed P-3C Orion. A turboprop aircraft developed from an exceptionally humdrum civil airliner called the Electra, it was an archetypal ugly duckling. The strong and roomy airframe, reliable flying characteristics and good endurance were a sound basis for developments in avionics, data-gathering and attack abilities that have proved attractive to a dozen nations' maritime forces. It is evolutionary in the best tradition of American technology, updates succeeding one another at intervals of only a few years.

The operational heart of the aircraft is its processing equipment, into which all the sensor information is fed. The latest update incorporates the Proteus digital computer which, it is claimed, does the tiresome chores, which previously had to be carried out manually, to the extent that more than 80% of the crew's time is now available for decision-making as opposed to number-crunching. In particular it produces the all-important localisation and tracking solutions on which the computation of the attack data – also done by the Proteus – depends. It will also be capable of incorporating data from non-sonic sources organic to the aircraft, and from external sources via a data link. By the same means it can transmit its data, both current and memorised, to other units.

The organic sources that feed the processor are quite numerous. The fundamental one, without which nothing else can make sense, is the aircraft's position and movement. This, with the aid of both

Table 8: Fixed Wing AS Aircraft: Shore-Based

Type	Country of origin	Length	Wingspan	Speed	Max take-off weight	Engines	Range with 2 hr on patrol(1)	Remarks
Atlantique 2	France	110ft 4in (33.63m)	122ft 9in (37.42m)	Mach .73	97,665lb (44,300kg)	2×4225Kw Rolls-Royce Tyne MK2c	1,800nm	42 ordered for French Navy. ASW load 4×Mark 46 torpedoes, 78 sonobuoys. Succeeds Atlantique 1, still operated by Germany, Italy, Pakistan and Netherlands.
Kawasaki UP-2J	USA/ Japan	91ft 8in (27.94m)	103ft 11in (31.50m)	240kt		2×Wright + 2×turbo-jet	1,000nm	Typical derivative of Neptune P-2 of which many versions still operate.
Be-12 (Mail)	USSR	99ft 0in (30.17m)	97ft 6in (29.71m)	328kt	64,925lb (29,450kg)	2×3,124Kw Ivchenko AI-20D	800nm	ISD 1961. Flying boat.
Il-38 (May)	USSR	129ft 10in (39.60m)	122ft 8in (37.40m)	347kt	–	4×3,124Kw Ivchenko AI-20D	1,500nm	Carries MAD, sonobuoys and AS weapons. Also operated by Indian Navy
TU-95 (Bear F)	USSR	162ft 5in (49.50m)	167ft 8in (51.10m)	500kt	414,470lb (188,000kg)	4×11,033Kw Kuznetsov NK-12MV	2,600nm	In Service 1973. Two large stores bays for sonobuoys and weapons.
Nimrod Mark 2	UK	126ft 9in (38.63m)	114ft 10in (35.00m)	500kt	177,500lb (80,510kg)	4×Rolls-Royce Spey Mark 250	2,100nm	ISD 1980. Up to 9 torpedoes in bomb bay. Sonobuoys stowed internally.
Orion P-3C	USA	116ft 10in (35.61m)	99ft 8in (30.37m)	410kt	135,000lb (61,235kg)	4×3,361Kw Allison T56-A-14	1,500nm	ISD 1969. Up to 8 torpedoes. Operated by 10 navies.

Note
(1). The 'Range with 2hr on patrol' column is an attempt to standardise on a single parameter a mass of diverse data on range, speed and endurance. It should be regarded as an indication of relative capability rather than an absolute figure.

inertial and doppler sensors, is a great deal more accurate nowadays than it was 25 years ago, when after one large-scale exercise out of sight of land the writer calculated the average navigational error, on aircraft-generated submarine datums, as just over 10 miles. But after this basic input, the one that is operationally most important is that from sonobuoys and these require a paragraph of their own.

The simplest type of sonobuoy is passive and non-directional; the most common in United States Naval service is the Sparton AN/SSQ-41B. It is operated by a seawater-activated battery and its other essential components are a hydrophone and a radio transmitter by which the received sound signals are passed to the aircraft. Descent is parachute-retarded. Once the buoy enters the water, the hydrophone descends to either a shallow

Right:
A submarine-launched anti-ship missile: the necessary scope of anti-submarine operations is greatly increased by this development.
Crown Copyright

or deep position as determined by the water conditions and set by the ubiquitious computer. Data is transmitted on a preset VHF channel, one of 31 available. The sonic range is 10Hz – 2.4KHz. Responses show up, after processing by fast Fourier transform techniques, as spectral lines on the cathode ray tubes or 'hard copy' equipment. Once responses have been identified from one or more non-directional buoys, directional buoys (DIFAR) may be laid to refine and track the contact. The standard DIFAR buoy is the AN/SSQ-53, though a deep-water buoy with a reputed capability for long-range detection is being introduced in the AN/SSQ-77A. For attack solutions, active sonobuoys may be used. These incorporate a low-power transmitter of sound pulses which can of course provide range information on any echo it receives. American buoys are divided into three types: an automatically-transmitting non-directional buoy, providing range information only, the AN/SSQ-47; a command-activated buoy that transmits only when keyed by the aircraft, the AN/SSQ-50B; and a directional command-activated buoy, the AN/SSQ-62B. Finally in this catalogue of American buoys, one must not forget the bathythermograph buoy, a provider of the basic thermal information on which so much depends. Being interpreted, it will tell the operators in the aircraft at what depth the sonobuoy transducers should be set to make the best use of the water conditions.

Other information available to the aircraft will include MAD responses, used only for confirmation at a very late stage in the ASW process for fear of alerting the submarine by the necessary low pass over it; low-light television or forward-looking infra-red equipments; electronic support equipment which might possibly detect a submarine's cautiously-used radar; and the radar of the aircraft itself. It is not often that one hears Americans coveting British equipment, but the P-3Cs' crews do have great admiration for the British Searchwater radar.

Top:
A P-3 Orion anti-submarine aircraft.
US Navy Official photograph

Above:
A very far cry from modern aircraft navigation: these instruments were in use until the middle 1950s and their replacement by doppler and inertial systems has vastly improved positional accuracy.
Crown Copyright

The P-3C crew consists of three pilots, a navigator, TACCO, two flight engineers, three sensor operators, an ordnanceman and an in-flight technician. Crew changes are more rapid than squadron commanders would like, and particular efforts are made to keep the operational nucleus of aircraft commander, TACCO and senior acoustic and non-acoustic operators together.

If the P-3C was developed from a very ordinary airliner, the British Nimrod was developed from a very special one. The Comet, from which it derives, was after all by a long way the world's first jet airliner, and its elegant configuration, with the engines mounted in the wingroots, is still apparent even in the latest version, the Nimrod 2. The

Top:
An Aurora P-3 derivative of the Canadian Air Force
Crown Copyright

Above:
A Nimrod Mk 2 of the Royal Air force. Note the refuelling probe in the nose. First fitted for the South Atlantic campaign, they have improved flexibility in general. *Crown Copyright*

elegance extends to the interior, as the writer discovered when, on his last day in uniform, he flew by courtesy of the Royal Air Force in one of these impressive aircraft.

Again, the central processor is the operational heart of the aircraft. In this case it is the Marconi AQS-901, a digital processing and display system that is exceptionally clear in presentation as well as quick and accurate in operation. Navigational input comes from the Tactical Aircraft Navigation System (TANS), into which waypoints can be injected, greatly facilitating the execution of searches and patrols. (The Mark 5 Sea King helicopters have this system too, and their crews find it a great boon). The sonobuoy inputs are very well presented for analysis both in cathode-ray and hard-copy versions, and can then be transferred automatically to the tactical display for plan presentation, localisation, tracking and attack.

The sonobuoy sensors are similar to those produced in the United States, but the basic non-directional buoy, the miniature Jezebel, covers even lower sonic frequencies than its American counterpart. Moreover, the directional buoy, called the Barra and developed in Australia, is of advanced design with a hydrophone array that uses beam steering techniques and transmits its information in digital form. Two active buoys are available, the non-directional SSQ-947B Ranger and the new directional command-activated multi-beam sonobuoy (CAMBS) whose transducer depth can be varied by command from the aircraft.

MAD and, shortly, forward-looking infra-red installations will be available as adjuncts to the

Table 9: Sonobuoys

Designation	Country of origin	Mode	Acoustic freq. range	Depth settings	Operating life	RF channels	Remarks
AN/SSQ-36	USA	Bathy	–	to 1,000ft (305m)	12min	–	
AN/SSQ-57	USA	Passive non-directional	–	to 1,000ft (305m)	1,3 or 8hr	31	Measures ambient noise
AN/SSQ-41	USA	Passive non-directional	10Hz-10KHz	65ft (20m) or 1,000 ft (305m)	1, 3 or 8hr	31	Most commonly used LOFAR buoy
DSTV-4M	France	Passive non-directional	10Hz-2.4KHz	65ft (20m) or 325ft (100m) or 1,000ft (300m)	1, 3 or 8 hr	99	Miniature version available
Jezebel	UK	Passive non-directional	5Hz-5KHz	60ft (18m) or 300ft (90m) or 450ft (137m)	1, 4 or 8hr	99	Miniature version available
SSQ 517/8	Canada	Passive non-directional	10Hz-10KHz	–	–	–	
AN-SSQ-53B	USA	Passive directional	10Hz 2.4KHz	88ft (27m) or 1,000ft (305m)	1 or 4hr	99	Three-element array
AN-SSQ-77A	USA	Passive directional	10Hz 2.4KHz	–	–	–	11-element vertical array
SSQ-801 Barra	Australia	Passive directional	10Hz-2KHz	82ft(25m) or 440ft (135m)	30min to 9hr	99	Digital transmission
AN/SSQ-47	USA	Active non-directional	–	60ft (18m) or 800ft (244m)	30min	12	Automatic keying
AN/SSQ-50B	USA	Active non-directional	–	60ft (18m) or 1,500ft (457m)	30min or 1hr	31	Command activated
AN-SSQ-62B	USA	Active directional	–	60ft (18m) or 1,500ft (457m)	30min or 1hr	31	Command activated
AN/SSQ-75	USA	Passive	–	Very deep	–	–	Expendable reliable acoustic path buoy. Under development.
SSQ-522	Canada	Active non-directional	–	60ft(18m) or 818ft (250m)	30min	12	Developed from AN/SSQ-47
SSQ-523 Cancass	Canada	Active non-directional	–	60ft (18m) or 818ft (250m)	30min	12	Command activated
SSQ-947B Ranger	UK	Active non-directional	13-19 KHz	–	30min	–	Automatic keying
CAMBS	UK	Active directional	–	–	–	31	Command activated

other sensors. But the greatest pride of the Nimrod 2 sensor suite is the Searchwater radar. Very accurate and sensitive, with digital inputs into the central tactial system, it gives impressively detailed information not only on the presence and position of targets but on their size and inclination. Its expected ranges on submarine periscopes and snorts are classified but are certainly enough to give any conventional submarine commander grave concern.

Crews of these aircraft are clearly delighted with what they have got, particularly now that in-flight refuelling facilities are being fitted so that range can be extended. The aircraft are flown with élan - once in contact with a submarine, they spend much of their time on one wingtip, seldom straying more than a couple of miles from the quarry – and operated with a good understanding of the capabilities and limitations of the equipment. There are limitations, of course; things are happening very fast and the necessary accuracy, particularly for a successful attack, depends on everything being right. One sonobuoy giving inconsistent information can spoil one's entire day.

France also produces a fixed-wing shore-based aircraft, the Bréguet Atlantique, of which a second generation is soon to enter service. All the equipment is French designed and made, the main contractor being Thomson-CSF. Sonobuoys are of the same general categories as those aleady described, and the sonobuoy processor system is built up from two TSM-8210 Salang computers each of which can handle signals from two active and eight passive sonobuoys. The French have an interesting MAD development using a new principle, the measurement of nuclear magnetic resonance with electronic pumping. It is claimed that this gives significant advantages in easy maintenance, low power consumption, quick start-up and simplicity over the conventional optical pumping system.

Canada is also active in the sonobuoy field. A whole family of sonobuoys is produced by Sparton Canada for Canadian Navy and RCAF requirements, and the Calypso lightweight acoustic processor is also unique to the Canadian Forces.

Soviet fixed-wing ASW is something of an enigma. At least three types of aircraft are known to be configured for ASW operations: the BE-12 flying boat (code-name 'Mail'), an Il-62 variant ('May') and a Tu-95 variant ('Bear F'). By the standards of maritime patrol aircraft, these are of short, medium and long range respectively. They have the external characteristics of such aircraft; large bomb bays that also carry sonobuoys, MAD booms and so forth. But little is known of their sensor and weapon fits; if there are some in the West who do know, they keep it to themselves, probably rightly. It is a fair deduction from everything else that is known about Soviet naval practice that their equipment will be physically relatively large, sturdy in construction and simple in operation. Where they do go for electronically sophisticated systems, they will try to keep men out of the loop completely. Soviet maritime patrol aircraft have not, so far as is known, conducted intensive surveillance operations against any Western submarine.

Lightweight Torpedo

The lightweight homing torpedo is now an ubiquitous weapon for launching from surface ships, light and heavy helicopters, and fixed-wing aircraft. The idea of a self-homing acoustic-headed

torpedo was already about early in World War 2, and actually went to sea in the German 'Gnat' in 1943; but this of course was an anti-ship, not an anti-submarine device and was for firing from submarines. It was not until nearly a decade later that the techniques involved could be developed enough to make them available for a lightweight air-portable torpedo that could be used against submarines.

First in the field was the United States with the Mark 44, which came into service in the early 1950s and is still very widely deployed throughout the Western world. Powered by a sea-water battery, the torpedo relies on a built-in active sonar for detection of its target. It must therefore be dropped in, or be directed to, a position close enough to the target where, after carrying out a first search pattern, it can acquire it with its own sonar. It is reasonable to assume that the necessary precision will be hundreds rather than thousands of yards. Later torpedoes are claimed to be less depth-limited, which suggests that the Mark 44's crushing depth is not very great.

The next US lightweight torpedo was the Mark 46. Similar in dimensions to the Mark 44, so that the two are virtually interchangeable on a number of different carrying vehicles, this has both passive and active acoustic homing, which almost certainly gives it greater flexibility and more margin for error in the dropping point. There have been several important modifications during the torpedo's life: Otto fuel instead of the sea-water battery, improved homing logic, better shallow water performance presumably through the refinement of anti-clutter circuitry, the ability to dive deeper, and improvement in active sonar performance that should restore ranges to the levels at which they stood before the Russians started to apply anechoic coatings to their submarine hulls. The latest version, nicknamed 'Neartip', is thus an effective torpedo against current submarine threats, but the US is continuing development of an advanced lightweight torpedo (ALWT), which will have an enlarged target detection envelope and better speed and endurance.

Meanwhile Britain, which had been using American torpedoes since the late 1950s, was developing her own advanced design, now called Stingray. Search and homing modes are both

Table 10: Lightweight Torpedoes

Designation	Country of origin	Length	Dia	Weight	Homing Mode	Remarks
L4	France	10ft 3in (313cm)	21in	1,188lb (540kg)	Active	Circular search. Contact and acoustic proximity fuze.
A244/S	Italy	8ft 10in (270cm)	12¾in (324mm)	–	Active/passive with countermeasures	Electric propulsion. Self-adaptive search patterns with a wide range of options claimed.
Type 42	Sweden	8ft 5in (262cm)	15¾in (400mm)	638lb (290kg)	Wire guidance available. Passive homing.	Ship or helicopter launch
Stingray	UK	7ft 11in (210cm)	13in (330mm)	–	Passive/active	Powerful propulsion and very high single shot kill probability claimed.
Mark 44	USA	8ft 6in (260cm)	12¾in (324mm)	432lb (196kg)	Active	
Mark 46	USA	8ft 6in (260cm)	12¾in (324mm)	506lb (230kg)	Passive/active	Later versions have Otto fuel and improved homing logic.
ALWT	USA	–	12¾in (324mm)	–	Passive/active	Speed about 40kt. Directed energy warhead to improve lethality. Mark 46 replacement.

passive and active, using sophisticated beam-forming techniques. The responses are fed into an onboard computer of great capacity and flexibility. The software which can be put into the computer, and kept up to date as intelligence and experience allow, should ensure that false targets, whether fortuitous or deliberately released by the submarine, are rejected. Excellent deep and shallow water performance is claimed, and the computer will even tell its torpedo what sonar modes and attack tactics to adopt.

France, Sweden and Italy all produce lightweight torpedoes. The French L4 is the only one of similar girth to submarine-launched torpedoes; this makes it heavier than the others, and it has been less successful in export markets than many French equipments. A new lightweight torpedo, the NTL/90, is under development by the French Ministry of Defence. The Italians, on the other hand, have scored a success with the Whitehead-Motofides A-244. Of similar configuration to the Mark 46 and with electric propulsion, it has a passive/active homing head, the latest version of which is claimed to have very advanced countermeasures against acoustic deception. Finally, the Swedish Type 42 is an electrically-powered passive homer. One significant feature of this torpedo strikes the eye: the warhead is of 50lb weight.

This pinpoints one problem of lightweight torpedoes. By their very nature they are incapable of carrying a large warhead. There are various ways of maximising the lethality of a small one: it can be set to go off at a certain distance from a submarine's hull, and not on impact, which increases the shock; it can be specially configured, again to maximise the shock effect; and the torpedo logic can be refined to seek out vulnerable points of the submarine.

Nevertheless the Soviet Navy is clearly seeking to present the West with physically very tough submarine targets; and the more the West is driven to devices such as those described, the more there is to go wrong.

If there is one thing that worries me more about this chancy business of anti-submarine warfare than any other, it is the West's reliance on torpedoes as killing weapons. It bears repeating that as a ready weapon at the start of a conflict, the torpedo's record is appalling. It has been no surprise to hear so many colleagues preface or end any comment on torpedoes with 'As long as it works on the day. . .' Of course we are much less lax about trials and operational reliability than were several nations before World War 2. The test facilities at AUTEC in the Bahamas, and off Hawaii, are comprehensive and well used, and the criteria are realistic and rigorous. Nevertheless I still find myself wishing that

the West had more ways of plastering the sea with high explosive, which is at the very least a deterrent to a submarine, particularly at long ranges. If these are not available there will be a tendency, after a few torpedo failures, for commanders to press for release of the cruder and more politically inflammatory anti-submarine weapon, the nuclear depth bomb.

Nuclear Weapons

Almost any vehicle that is capable of carrying a torpedo can be adapted to take a nuclear charge. The Soviet Union is known to have one missile system, the FRAS-1, designed specially for nuclear ASW; but the more common SS-N-14 has also a capability in the kiloton range, giving a lethal radius of the order of a mile round the point of impact, and is can be assumed that Soviet helicopters can carry nuclear depth bombs of a similar sort. In the West, the W55 nuclear depth bomb can be carried in long range maritime patrol aircraft and heavy helicopters, and is the warhead of the SUBROC missile system which will be described in a later section of this chapter. The W55 is an American device and is owned by other countries on a dual-key basis.

Political considerations would of course figure very prominently in any decision whether or not to use nuclear ASW weapons at sea, and would be particularly acute if first use was involved. It would be necessary for a commander-in-chief, on the NATO side, to convince the high political command that the need was overwhelming; and although some Kremlin-watchers would argue that in Russia these things are left more to the military, my guess is that on the day the Politburo's sanction would be required on the Soviet side. Nevertheless there is some difference between the use of nuclear weapons at sea and on land that makes the former marginally more likely. It is significant that of all the nuclear weapons known to be in existence, the W55 is the only one that does not appear in the tables of the International Institute for Strategic Studies' publication *The Military Balance*: a symptom, perhaps, of the attitude which regards any form of nuclear warfare on land as highly sensitive because it involves people, while nuclear warfare at sea concerns only sailors.

Submarines

It is often put forward as a self-evident truth, and not only by submariners, that the submarine is the best anti-submarine vehicle. But the realities of anti-submarine warfare have had a way in the past of deflating claims, particularly claims of simple and obvious solutions, and so such statements cannot pass without critical examination.

The nuclear-powered submarine certainly has great merits as an anti-submarine vessel. It is, first, a natural player of the bathymetric game, being able to position itself at the optimum depth, consistent with its own hull limitations, for detecting opposing submarines. Moreover, in a one-to-one contest between two submarines of precisely equal capability and training, the one that has a job to do other than anti-submarine work – that is to say transitting, moving into position to attack surface forces, or establishing communication with the outside world – is more vulnerable because it cannot operate at the optimum sonic state; it has to go faster, or at another depth, than it would like.

Another merit of the submarine as an anti-submarine vehicle, and this again applies particularly to the nuclear-powered boat, lies in its excellent electrical power supplies. Not only do these allow for powerful active sonar when needed but they also give ample supply to sophisticated data processing and weapon control equipment. Good weapon control is of course particularly important in the underwater battle because of the relatively slow pace of underwater vehicles, and here the ability of a submarine to guide its torpedoes by wire towards their targets, so reducing dead time to a minimum, is a great asset. Finally, the sea endurance of all classes of submarine – even a conventionally-powered boat can easily sustain a patrol of over two months without any logistic support – is a great point in their favour.

It is often claimed that a submarine's 'invulnerability' in hostile waters is a clinching argument in its favour as a prime ASW vehicle. There is some logical inconsistency here; if submarines are invulnerable one had better stop talking about ASW. And in a transit towards hostile waters, like the Barents Sea, a submarine will have to run some gauntlets; Soviet barrier concepts are similar to the West's, and their resources are improving. It is well known that they set great store by the 'bastions' in the northern seas, and air and surface opposition throughout those areas is likely to be heavy. Nevertheless it is quite right to say that a submarine is the only ASW vehicle that could be sent into such waters with a realistic chance of survival; and that its employment would tie up a significant number of opposing forces.

It is these qualities that have led the British and US navies, in particular, to set anti-submarine warfare as the highest priority in their submarine operations. But the submarine does have demerits as an anti-submarine warfare vehicle too. First, if it tries to go too fast, in an attempt to gain a favourable tactical position, it exposes itself to detection; so there is a constant trade-off between mobility and detectability. Second, and probably

more important, is the question of information and communication. When submerged, a submarine will know what its passive sensors tell it; they may not be anything like the whole of what it needs to know. A submariner who thinks he has the whole picture is probably in a fool's paradise. But to gain more information the boat must pay a penalty in coming shallow to listen for radio communication; and if he wants this to be two-way it may have to be shallower still. Finally, and linked with the former point, there is the question of identification friend or foe. Ideally the submariner likes to operate in a patrol area where he can treat everything that moves as hostile and where he has reasonable grounds for believing he will not be attacked by friendly forces. It is not at all easy for the command authorities to organise things thus, and even if they do (restricting the activities of other ASW units accordingly) mistakes can occur.

Probably behind the claims for the submarine as an anti-submarine vehicle lies the hidden assumption the 'ours are better than theirs'. In particular this would apply to quietness, the sensitivity and accuracy of sensors, the effectiveness of weapons and the state of training. Until recently

there was remarkable unanimity in the West on this point: ours were better than theirs, in all these fields. In the past two or three years, however, there has been a distinct change of tone from the commentators, a suggestion that while the Russians have not caught up yet, the West's lead in submarine technology and operation is being eroded at many points. In particular, they may be better at things the West has not bothered about much; and they may be prepared to use methods of comparative crudity that the West has, because of its emphasis on quality and precision, not comtemplated.

Nevertheless the West has by all accounts a current lead. Even in submarine numbers it does not compare badly; NATO has almost as many as the Soviet Union, and certainly they are trained more predominantly in the submarine-versus-submarine role. Many of them will be operating in waters they know well, and some of the less experienced Soviet crews will not have that advantage. This cuts both ways, of course; the fact that Italian, or Turkish submarines are most unlikely to operate beyond the Mediterranean limits NATO's flexibility.

So far as material is concerned, the quality of NATO's varies considerably. Most of the boats are of modern design, including the conventionals which NATO European navies operate but which the US Navy, notably, do not. Many of them are small but this is not necessarily a disadvantage; indeed, by Argentine accounts the German-built 1,000ton *San Luis* survived her patrol in the area of the British Task Force in 1982 principally because she was small, had a low noise signature and used the continental shelf waters well. Small size does, however, tend to reduce patrol endurance, and clearly very powerful active sonars are out of the question.

The conventional submarines generally carry British, French, German or Italian torpedoes (it is astonishing how the torpedo, a high development risk if ever there was one, attracts countries with relatively limited armaments industries). These are all of the standard 21in (533mm) diameter with ranges of the order of 10 miles (16km) and speeds of about 30kt. The fact that they are wire-guided in midcourse and have acoustic terminal homing heads probably works against higher speeds being employed.

Three Western navies now operate nuclear-powered fleet submarines. Last into the field was France, whose nuclear power programme had been reserved for the top-priority ballistic missile submarine force. The first nuclear attack boat, *Rubis*, was therefore not launched until 1979. One

Below:
Western nuclear-powered submarines are conceived as anti-submarine platforms. The launch of HMS *Turbulent*. *British Shipbuilders photograph*

Table 11: Heavyweight Torpedoes

Designation	Country of origin	Length	Dia	Weight	Homing Mode	Remarks
L5	France	–	21in (533mm)	2,200lb 1,000kg	Passive/active	Mod 3 is 660lb (300kg) heavier Direct attack or programmed search and attack. Speed 35kts.
Seeschlange	Germany	13ft 1in (400cm)	21in (533mm)	–	Wire-guided, Passive/active	Three-dimensional sonar. Attack can be completed by the ship, or autonomously. Electric propulsion, selectable speed.
A184	Italy	19ft 8in (600cm)	21in (533mm)	2,860lb (1,300kg)	Wire-guided, panoramic Passive/active	Range over 8.7nm (14km). Wire guidance and two-way communication to point of acquisition by torpedo.
Type 61	Sweden	23ft 0in (702cm)	21in (533mm)	3,883lb (1,765kg)	Wire-guided	Hydrogen peroxide propulsion. Long range
Mark 24 Tigerfish	UK	21ft 2in (646cm)	21in (533mm)	3,410lb (1,550kg)	Wire-guided, Passive/active	Two-speed electric motor. Impact and proximity fuze. To be succeeded by Spearfish (NST/R7525)
NT 37D	USA	14ft 9in (451cm)	19in (483mm)	1,650lb (750kg)	Passive/active	Not wire-guided; three preset search modes. Incremental improvements continue. Dimensions of later versions vary.
Mark 48	USA	19ft 0in (580cm)	21in (533mm)	3,474lb (1,579kg)	Wire-guided, passive/active	55kt speed, 23½ mile (38km) range reported. Otto fuel.
ADCAP	USA	–	21in (533mm)	–	–	Mark 48 successor. Expanded operating envelope.

would hesitate to call her a first-generation boat, but her small size and low reported speed suggest that the specification was deliberately unambitious and it is not certain how firmly it is based on anti-submarine warfare. French submarine sonar suites do not at present seem to include towed arrays.

The British have of course been in the game nearly 20 years longer, and now have 13 fleet submarines in commission. They show a steady, evolutionary improvement which one can assume has concentrated particularly on quietening, sensor performance, diving depth, endurance, manoeuvrability and maintainability.

The Royal Navy is more sensitive than any other, except the Soviet, about disclosing the capabilities of its nuclear submarines and particularly their sonar sensors. They are claimed to be 'advanced', and the use of towed arrays has been mentioned in the recruiting literature. The associated weapons are rather better publicised. The boats carry very large torpedo outfits of over 20 weapons with fast reloading of their five tubes. Several different types of torpedo are carried but the main anti-submarine weapon is the Mark 24 Tigerfish. This is an electrically driven torpedo which is wire-guided throughout most of its run; the submarine's instruments work out a lead angle so that an intercepting course is steered. During the self-homing phase the torpedo's on board computer interprets the data from the homing head's passive/active senors and works out the course to steer, subject to a command override from the submarine.

The Spearfish, an advanced heavy anti-submarine torpedo using many of the techniques of the Stingray, is under development.

The United States, with some 90 nuclear-powered attack submarines, is the chief NATO provider in this field (though of course a proportion of the boats are assigned to the Pacific Fleet). The most numerous classes are the 'Sturgeons', built in the decade around 1970, and the class of much bigger and more expensive 'Los Angeles' boats which are still in production.

Clearly the US Navy has gone for submarine-towed passive sonar arrays in a big way. The 'Los Angeles' class are said all now to be fitted with the AN/BQQ-5 outfit which is a digital, multi-beam system employing both hull-mounted and towed hydrophones. The towed body will be at the end of a maximum of 2,500ft (800m) of cable. It is claimed that significantly greater ranges than were previously attainable can now be obtained on Soviet submarines, at higher search rates, and that on one occasion two Soviet Victor class submarines were tracked simultaneously.

At present the standard weapon fit is perhaps not quite up with the sensor capabilities. The long-range weapon is the SUBROC, an air-flight nuclear-headed missile that swims out of a torpedo tube in an underwater launch. It is nearly 20 years since it first deployed and a new weapon, the Common ASW stand-off weapon (also for fitting in surface ships) is under development. It will be available for over-the-horizon targeting, via the comprehensive 'Outlaw Shark' information system, as well as for use with the submarine's own sensors, and will carry an advanced lightweight torpedo or a nuclear depth bomb. The heavy, tube-launched system at present is the Mark 48, which in its Mod 3 version is Otto-fuelled and has an active/passive homing head that takes over after the wire guidance phase. The successor now planned is the advanced capability (ADCAP) torpedo with a forecast range of 24 miles (38km) and a speed of 55kt.

Soviet submarine-versus-submarine capability, and the uncertainties surrounding it, have already been briefly discussed. It would be in line with Soviet philosophy if they attempted to co-ordinate the activities of several submarines against a single target, but this would require good underwater communication and may not yet be within their grasp. Weaponry now includes a SUBROC-type weapon, the SS-N-15, as well as nuclear-headed torpedoes.

Mines

In both world wars Britain conducted a wide-ranging mining campaign against U-boats. Their port approaches were mined; a barrage was laid across the Dover Strait; surface patrols and convoy routes endeavoured to divert submarines into 'trap' minefields; and in World War 2 a mammoth barrier, absorbing over 30% of the 260,000 mines laid in that war, was established across the Greenland-Iceland-UK gaps.

The Dover Strait barrage had the most effect in denying a short and convenient route for small U-boats to the Channel. Port approach minefields sank a few submarines and caused the Germans to put much effort into minesweeping. Trap minefields were too inflexible, unresponsive to changes in the enemy's dispositions and indeed to our own. The barrage in the gaps sank only one submarine; the Germans regarded it as ineffective, and ignored it.

Against a Soviet submarine threat all the methods quoted would be available, but in the very flexible operational pattern, trap minefields would probably be even less effective than before. Given the Soviet watch on their port approaches, mining them could scarcely be accomplished by any unit other than a submarine. Moreover, the Soviet Navy has a very large mine-sweeping force which presumably is designed to cope with all the kinds of influence mine – magnetic, acoustic, pressure – available to the West. Narrow and relatively shallow straits not under Soviet surveillance could very profitably be mined, and there is no doubt that the Danish and Turkish navies are equipped for this purpose.

Mining in the broader and deeper ocean gaps is potentially the most important and most controversial. It has been made so by the invention of an entirely new kind of mine, the CAPTOR (Captive Torpedo). This is a bottom-laid device which has two main components. The first is a detection and control unit which, once activated, listens for noise from submarines; it is gated to ignore surface traffic. Once a submarine is heard at sufficient intensity, a mechanism is triggered which releases the second component, a Mark 46 torpedo. This rises to the optimum operating depth and starts a search, attacking the submarine when it gains contact. It is claimed that CAPTOR has an effective blocking width of about a mile and a kill probability as high as 0.3.

Since the unit cost is said to be about £100,000, a field of say 1,000 mines in the Greenland-Iceland-UK gaps would represent excellent value for money if these claims are true. £100 million to achieve an attrition rate of 30% is a small price to pay by current standards. But the CAPTOR is a very complicated system and has been through intense development problems. There is the question not only of innate reliability, but of reliability after being on the bottom for a long period of time. It appears that after long evaluation the United States Navy is satisfied on these points; at any rate, CAPTOR is in production and is regarded as an in-service weapon. It does, of course, preclude the operations of Western submarines in areas where it is laid and raises, therefore, one more major problem of water space management.

A word ought to be said about mining as a counter to non-Soviet submarine threats. Most small submarine forces operate from but a single base, and minesweeping and surveillance effort is likely to be light and unsophisticated. A quite small blockading minefield laid by a submarine could be highly cost-effective in bottling up an opposing submarine force and, perhaps, eliminating escalation in that particular field.

The Soviet Union has a very large stock of mines and it is likely that a proportion of them would be laid for anti-submarine purposes, particularly to prevent infiltration off Soviet port approaches and to inhibit deployment of Western ballistic missile submarines from their bases. While all the usual actuation devices for ground mines are certainly available to the Soviet Navy, their access to CAPTOR-type mines is by no means so sure. It would be in character for them to want to diversify the threat but not to complicate their own equipment too much, so that some sort of rising mine that is clever, but not too clever, can be predicted.

Exotic ASW Measures

The fact that the submarine-based deterrent has been claimed to be virtually invulnerable is probably responsible for the more fanciful flights of fiction, typically theories of space-based lasers dealing out instant destruction to submarines detected by infra-red emissions. There does not seem to be any justification for James Bond speculation of this sort. But the amount of research now going on in the anti-submarine field suggests that some new measures will carry on the painstaking, incremental improvement against an increasing threat that is the history of this form of warfare throughout the century.

Data-gathering on submarines may increasingly make use of non-acoustic means. On the parallel of Fast Fourier Transforms in the acoustic field, the processing of very small, satellite-detected anomalies in ocean waves or temperature could possibly yield results with an acceptable false-alarm rate. The road will be difficult and signposted For Superpowers Only.

The same restriction may well apply to unconventional hull forms for surface ships. Hovercraft or surface effect vessels are not, on analysis, particularly suitable for anti-submarine work; their closeness to the surface denies them the aircraft's wide area coverage and ability to monitor sonobuoy fields, their towing power is not great and it is hard to envisage a suitable mode of ocean operation involving hull-mounted or dipping sonar. They do have excellent resistance to underwater explosions but in an age when submarines can deploy air-flight missiles this is not so important as it used to be. More potential for anti-submarine work may be found in the small waterplane area twin-hull ship (SWATH). This consists essentially of two deep catamaran (or shallow submarine) hulls joined by an above-water superstructure that can operate aircraft, carry air defence systems and provide command and control. Its stability is in theory much superior to that of a monohull and it should make an

Below:
Decoy and deception are part of the anti-submarine battle. A noisemaker to seduce anti-ship acoustic torpedoes. *Crown Copyright*

excellent platform not only for aircraft but for complex and powerful hull-mounted sonar, which ASW forces may increasingly need if submarine quietening outstrips the abilities of passive sensors. But development of SWATH is likely to be very expensive, beyond the means of medium powers.

Two aircraft of unconventional design could have some future in ASW. Tilt-rotor machines, something between a helicopter and a fixed-wing aircraft, give faster forward speeds and therefore better reaction in datum investigation and co-operation with other units. And the so-called wing-in-ground (WIG) aircraft, which the Soviet Union has developed to some extent, does offer sprint-and-drift possibilities, though whether these would be in a more cost-effective form than those given by numerous other vehicles seems highly doubtful.

The airship, such a favoured ASW vehicle in World War 1 and by no means neglected in WW2, may be due for a resurgence at least in offshore ASW work. Two firms in the West, one in the UK and one in the USA, are busy on designs and prototypes, though without much government encouragement. The airship's advantages are its lofted sensors (which it shares with all aircraft) and endurance measured in days (which it does not). Its disadvantages are its low speed – dash speeds of about 60kt are standard – its relatively small payload and the need for unusual ground facilities.

The conventional mode for large-area bottom arrays has always been passive, and the advances in that field can only be incremental, though the flexibility given by rapidly-deployable air-laid systems (RDSS) and towed surveillance arrays (TAGOS) is welcome. Large-area active sonar bottom arrays would be a quite different development. Sometimes put forward by American enthusiasts, frequently misinterpreted and misquoted by the ignorant, 'the insonification of the ocean' by very powerful low-frequency active sonar located in the deep sound channel has superficial attractions. But the operational problems, particularly those of classification, are formidable. Reverberations, and echoes from the bottom, the surface and large marine life would tax any processing system beyond attainable limits. The effect on the proven passive systems could not be anything but degrading. The active systems themselves would be enormously expensive. Finally, the effect on marine life, particularly large mammals and fish, is unpredictable.

Mention of large marine mammals brings this chapter to an appropriate conclusion. Happily, experiments with sea-creatures as anti-submarine aids seem no longer to be conducted. Since the porpoise is, by some accounts, one of the very few advanced animals that is unable to harbour an aggressive thought in its head, long may it remain so.

The Anti-Submarine Battle

In this chapter it is intended to give some idea how NATO might fight the anti-submarine battle in the case of a major Soviet attack in Europe. The ideas are mine and are based on the material so far presented; Allied commanders may think differently and may have unpublished resources. So may the Russians. It needs to be said, too, that this case is not the only likely situation for major conflict, nor even the most likely. But it would be an exceptionally damaging sort of war for the West, and is therefore one which it particularly wants to deter and for which full preparation must be made. Because it comprehends all kinds of anti-submarine activity it makes the maximum demand on force structures and is therefore often called the 'determinant case' – the ultimate planning challenge. For the purpose of this book, this full gamut of operations gives the maximum illustrative value for the reader.

Western Objectives

A successful outcome for the West of this kind of war could not be less than the recovery of all territory taken by the Warsaw Pact in its initial assault. To achieve this it might not be necessary to retake all the territory by military means, but it would at least be necessary to demonstrate that the Warsaw Pact would suffer very badly until it was relinquished.

Given that overall objective it is not possible to imagine any rational NATO course of action that does not involve extensive use of the sea. The restoration of control on the Northern and Mediterranean flanks of the Alliance; the checking and turning round of the main assaults in Central Europe; the maintenance of control of NATO's islands; the continuance of essential supplies to Europe: all these need far too long a timescale, and far too massive a weight of material lift, to be dependent on air supplies or stockpiles. The theoretical short-run solution, the early use by NATO of theatre nuclear weapons, is not one that any NATO commander, much less minister, wants to rely on, since it risks a result in which everyone

has lost everything. So, if the use of the sea is relinquished, a successful outcome of any major NATO campaign is inconceivable.

Shall I say it again? I shall say it again, in even rounder terms: *If you plan any major NATO campaign without the use of the sea, you are planning to lose.*

What uses of the sea, then, will concern NATO in the determinant case? First, the ultimate strategic deterrent must be preserved; it underpins all the rest of the strategy, and in war it blocks off Soviet nuclear blackmail. Second, some threat must be posed to the Soviet strategic capability, to put doubt in the enemy's mind about his own ultimate power and to preoccupy his other naval forces. Third, control must be established in NATO's flank areas and other vital areas either in or adjacent to the sea. Fourth, reinforcements and supplies must come by sea to Western Europe, and must keep coming until a successful outcome is achieved.

Preservation of the Strategic Deterrent

For an open society, the West can be remarkably cagey when it wants to be. So it is no surprise to find very little information on how the USA, UK and France view the threat to their ballistic missile submarines, and even less on how they reckon to counter it. One falls back on informed speculation, and most of the source material for that comes from the Kremlin-watchers in the American institutes.

Western ballistic missile submarines carry out patrols of between two and three months at a time within range of their targets. They operate in a way calculated to avoid detection. In between patrols they must return to their bases, which are few, to replenish, carry out maintenance and change crews.

The dangerous focus of their activities is therefore their point of setting out on patrol. It is pretty well fixed in space (a glance at the chart of the Clyde approaches will give a fair illustration) and not unpredictable in time. Given the Soviet desire to counter all elements of what they regard as the Western threat, their forces can be expected to keep these approach areas under surveillance from

Above:
Preservation of the strategic deterrent must be an objective in war as well as peace. HMS *Revenge* in Scottish waters. *Crown Copyright*

surface craft – particularly the trawler-shaped intelligence collectors – and submarines, operating in international waters. If a Western ballistic missile submarine was detected going out on patrol, an attempt might be made to trail it, if the Soviets had a nuclear-powered boat in a position to do so. So far as is known, they have had no success so far in operations of this sort. And predictably, open-ocean searches for Western ballistic missile submarines have had no success either; the needle-in-a-haystack metaphor holds good absolutely.

This is the peacetime pattern and it is encouraging. However, in war it is likely that Soviet submarines would congregate in larger numbers around the strategic submarines' bases in the United Kingdom, France and the United States' eastern seaboard. Their rules of engagement might allow them to attack any Western submarine, and would almost certainly allow them to penetrate territorial waters. They would not have any help from surface craft; these, it must be assumed, would have been eliminated or withdrawn early in the war.

The West would have two problems, one politico-military and one purely military. In politico-military terms they would have to second-guess the Soviet rules of engagement and assess the volatility of the deterrent situation in the event of a full-scale battle round the bases. Probably, by means of public announcements and perhaps hot-line methods, it

could be made clear to the Russians that their submarines in such areas would be considered hostile and would be prosecuted to destruction, no less than in any other sea area; and that this could be done without detriment to strategic deterrence.

The military means for prosecuting such submarines would be organised by local shore commanders. The main assets used would be maritime patrol aircraft, co-operating in the offshore zone with nuclear submarines and in the inshore zone with shore-based helicopters and surface ships or coastal submarines as available. Off most of the strategic submarines bases there is deep water not far off shore, and this increases the part bottom arrays can play. Finally, against the submarine-laid mining threat a sophisticated minesweeping force must be available.

It cannot however be too much stressed that the ballistic missile submarine's main protection lies in its own qualities and mode of operation. Quiet that it may not be detected, quick and agile if necessary that it may not be localised or tracked, sturdy and well-equipped with weapons that it may not be killed, it should – so long as its technology remains in date – be more than a match for its opponents. It will do better still if its missile range gives it a greater amount of sea room in which to hide. All this is important because the West does not want to expend any more valuable resources than are absolutely necessary in de-lousing the areas round its strategic submarine bases.

Threatening the Soviet Strategic Submarine Force

Operations against the Soviet ballistic missile submarines are almost, but not quite, a mirror

image of theirs against ours. Western objectives would, it seems to me, be subtly different. They would be, first, to demonstrate to the Soviets that any attack they could mount against Western ballistic missile submarines would bring much more damaging retribution against their own; and, second, to ensure the preoccupation of a large proportion of the Soviet Navy's best and most modern units in the protection of their ballistic missile force, which is a point of doctrine they are known to hold particularly firmly.

Tactically, too, the mirror image is not exact. Because of the West's advantage in the sonic field, both technical and geographic, it does seem to me that it is worth taking the risk of defocusing the detection area from the immediate approaches to the Kola Inlet, particularly as Soviet surveillance of that area is likely to be extremely dense. NATO nuclear-powered submarines, therefore, could be expected to be working relatively far offshore, possibly towards the ice edge since the Russians are known to stress the importance of under-ice operation. They would have to be alert not only for Soviet surface and air ASW forces but for underwater escorts – it has been postulated that each 'Typhoon' might be ecorted by one 'Alfa' and one 'Victor-III' – and would be very much on their own. If SOSUS was still working, that might help; and it is just possible that surface forces in the Norwegian Sea might impinge on such operations. But by and large, this is the pure submarine-versus-submarine contest, conducted overwhelmingly by passive sonar, a game of hunt and ambush in the depths. It has never been done in battle. There are grounds for confidence in how any encounter might turn out, but the encounter rate itself is not, in my view, likely to be high.

It is possible that by mutual consent, and in the interest of preserving the stability of strategic deterrence, both sides would completely lay off each others' ballistic missile submarines in the early

stages of a war. The idea has been put forward often in the arms control context and probably commends itself to many people who do not regard themselves as part of the arms control lobby. The political and military establishments of the West would probably not find it too difficult to accept an agreement on these lines, so long as they were convinced that it would hold: the worst stumbling block would be the tactical minus of being unable to buy up Soviet resources by applying pressure at a spot the West knows to be sensitive. The Russians might have more difficulty, even though relinquishing the for them very difficult anti-Trident task would probably be to their overall advantage. They would have to make a very sharp shift in doctrine, away from war-fighting and towards deterrence, and they are not flexible in these matters.

Control on the Flanks and in Vital Sea Areas
The flanks of NATO are of immense importance to the Alliance for many reasons. In peace they are the homes of the sensitive outliers, Norway, Turkey and Greece, and the credibility of Allied deterrence

Above and left:
The Soviet Union places great emphasis on safe-guarding its strategic submarines, and may employ extensive surface and air ASW assets against any submarine threat to them. *Crown Copyright*

penetration for two reasons: first, because carrier-based aircraft could turn the military scale in this area; second, because they see an operational need for their own forces, including ballistic missile submarines, to use this stretch of water. For these reasons Nitze's committee in 1978 considered that '. . . the battle for the Norwegian Sea could be one of the major naval engagements of World War III'.

The forces on both sides would be large. Many American authorities have suggested that they would not attempt the contest with less than four carrier battle groups. The Soviet Navy would muster probably at least two 'Kiev'-class carriers under present conditions, and there are more to come; while shore-based aircraft from the north would pose a formidable stand-off missile threat. But it is with the anti-submarine battle that we are concerned.

In Chapter 2 I suggested that up to 20 guided missile submarines, and up to 40 with torpedo armament, might be available to the Soviet Union to contest the Norwegian Sea either in its approaches or in the Sea itself. They would attempt to co-ordinate their attacks not only with each other but with units of the Naval Air Force and the surface fleet; this concentration of force is central to Soviet doctrine and they appear ready to accept the problems of command, control and water space management associated with it.

In such circumstances an Allied combatant force has, in turn, a dilemma. Should it concentrate and accept a set-piece battle in the hope that, having won it, it could then get on with the job of flank support? Or should it seek from the start to disrupt enemy plans for concentration by being itself widely dispersed and freely manoeuvring? There might then be not so much a battle as a series of engagements, whose overall outcome would at first be hard to judge and whose duration might adversely affect performance in the primary task in support of the land battle.

My own inclination would be for the latter solution. The dispersal of Allied forces would be more apparent than real; the Norwegian Sea is only 1,000 miles by 800, margin to margin, and the scope of a single carrier battle group is nearly half that, so mutual support between dispersed groups would be considerable. The command, control and water space management problems would be greater in overall terms, but modern systems should be able to cope. And the plusses are enormous: the chance to confuse and deceive the opponent, to impose on him unwanted manoeuvre and exposure, to break up any set-piece plans he has, to scotch any chance of a killing ground where he could conceive of the use of shore-based ballistic missiles against the fleet. To advance with banners in review order invites the 'first salvo' which Gorshkov stresses so much in his teaching.

rests in large part on the assurance that can be given to them. In war they would almost certainly come under early attack, and if secured by the Soviet Union could be used as advanced bases from which to make further assaults. Conversely, if held by NATO, they would be a constant perceived menace to the Soviet Union, claws that could nip most sharply.

There is not space in this book to deal with both the Mediterranean and Norwegian Sea cases, so it will concentrate on the latter. To set the scene, it is worth recalling that in north Norway one Norwegian brigade faces seven Soviet divisions; that Norway allows no basing of foreign military formations or nuclear weapons on her soil in peacetime; and that northern Norway houses many Western surveillance installations.

It is in view of all this that NATO would fervently hope for a period of tension, short of actual hostilities, which lasted long enough to land reinforcements in Norway: Britain, Canada, the Netherlands and the United States could all be involved. If Allied troops could be landed and the main amphibious shipping withdrawn before hostilities started, the combatant forces' hands would be freed. If not, it would be very messy.

But whichever way it turned out, it seems likely that the Supreme Allied Commander Atlantic would see an operational need at some time to penetrate the Norwegian Sea with carrier strike forces, so that they could give air support to the northern flank; they might, in the worst case, have to support amphibious landings as well. The Soviet Union would be bound to oppose such a

Above:
Establishing control on the Northern Flank of NATO would be an important objective in any European conflict: Royal Marines exercising in North Norway.
Crown Copyright

The anti-submarine dispositions of each carrier battle group would accord with the principles that have been discussed in earlier chapters. An area of interest with a radius of about 300 miles is established in which submarine contacts, once identified as enemy, must be neutralised. Near the fringes of this zone the main effort will be from the air: shore-based aircraft from Norway, Iceland and Scotland and the carriers' own S-3 Vikings, using radar and sonobuoy searches. Closer in to the centre, passive sonar is still the main sensor, but deployed here by surface and submarine towed-array units, further supported by aircraft which in this case could be rotary as well as fixed-wing. In the inner zone, up to 15 or 20 miles from the high value units, active sonar becomes the major sensor and is deployed by surface ships and helicopters.

Further information on submarines may reach the group commander, via shore authorities, from sources such as SOSUS and independently-operating submarines and aircraft.

The question of who controls what, particularly towards the fringes of the area of interest, is an important one, and might become vital in a situation where communications had been badly disrupted by enemy action. Generally speaking, shore authorities, particularly those operating submarines

and maritime patrol aircraft, will prefer to retain control of their units rather than turn them over to seagoing commanders. But this will mean that their operations cannot readily be changed to meet new threats, nor to conform to variations in the movements or disposition of the force being supported; and if such changes are likely to be frequent it will be better for the seagoing commander to have control. Such questions can be investigated in peacetime exercises, and indeed that is one of their most important functions.

It is on the fringes of the area of interest, too, that operations will most likely impinge on adjacent areas. Here again command, control and communications are critical factors; it is absolutely necessary to confuse the enemy more than one confuses oneself. That applies equally to the movements of underway replenishment groups and amphibious forces. These will have their own close protection in the form of surface ships and perhaps helicopter carriers, Arapaho or otherwise, but will rely for more distant support on other forces.

Protection of Shipping
History and geography have conspired to ensure that the United States, with its Pacific experience in World War 2, its penchant for the overtly offensive, and its large resources, should emphasise above-water warfare and strike carrier operations, while the United Kingdom with its deep knowledge and experience of oceanic trade warfare, its sensitivity to the need for seaborne supplies and its aptitude for the tenacious holding battle, should emphasise anti-submarine warfare and shipping protection. That is why the previous section discussed the battle largely in terms of United States forces and resources, and why this section will be much more concerned with what the United Kingdom can do in the Eastern Atlantic. It is in this area that the United Kingdom provides some 70% of NATO's ready forces, a fair reflection of the distribution of interest, responsibility and expertise.

That expertise extends not only to the seagoing mechanics of trade warfare but to its administration. The British invented Naval Control of Shipping, the means by which merchant ships are organised for their protection, and have kept the art alive, mostly through dedicated reservists who give up their time for exercise and instruction. Not much money is spent on it; it has been a bit of a Cinderella;

Right:
Likely elements of a Soviet submarine threat in the Norwegian Sea. The 'Echo-II', *(below left)* **'Charlie'** *(centre)* **and 'Victor'** *(below right)* **classes are self-evident; no picture of the 'Oscar' was available at the time of going to press. The 'Kirov'** *(top)* **battle-cruiser is included because it may fulfil a critical seagoing command function.**
Crown Copyright

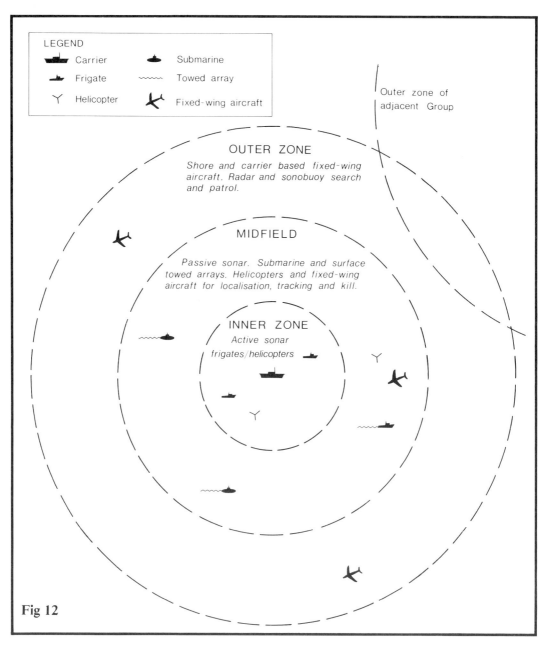

LEGEND

⊢ Carrier   ⊢ Submarine

⊢ Frigate   ∿∿∿ Towed array

Y Helicopter   ✈ Fixed-wing aircraft

Outer zone of
adjacent Group

OUTER ZONE

*Shore and carrier based fixed-wing
aircraft. Radar and sonobuoy search
and patrol.*

MIDFIELD

*Passive sonar. Submarine and surface
towed arrays. Helicopters and fixed-wing
aircraft for localisation, tracking and kill.*

INNER ZONE
*Active sonar
frigates/helicopters*

Fig 12

but if this Cinderella does not come to the ball, it will be over long before midnight.

Given, then, that merchant shipping can and will be organised for its own protection, how shall this be implemented at sea? The scale of the task has been assessed. Nitze's committee said that for military purposes – that is, to sustain the land-air battle – 200-300 nominal shiploads of dry cargo and 50 nominal 70,000 ton tanker loads of oil were needed each month. The immediate reinforcement requirement, before or at the start of hostilities, has been quoted as a million men and ten million tons of material. And for the economic needs of Europe in general, 1,000 cargoes a month are about standard.

Taken together these figures suggest rather over 40 merchant ships a day coming in to Western European ports from the Atlantic Ocean. How far east they would get depends on the state of the land war but the chances of say Hamburg being popular as a port of entry would clearly be low.

Against them, as discussed in Chapter 2, would be between 30 and 60 Soviet submarines, more if the

100

Fig 12
Carrier Battle Group anti-submarine measures. Note:
Not to scale. Numbers of units shows are purely
illustrative. The area will generally be moving, not
stationary, and units will operate in alloted sectors or
areas relative to the group centre.

Left:
Two organic elements of a US Carrier Battle Group:
S-3 Viking and 'Spruance' class destroyer.
US Navy Official photographs

readily redeployable. Moreover, there is some
evidence that units at low states of readiness were
counted in these numbers, while only the
immediately available units of the Soviet Navy were
so counted. Finally, the effect of the 30% cut then
planned in the number of surface ships in the Royal
Navy was not taken into account.

There is some suggestion in NATO reports that
merchant shipping would be routed well to the
south, particularly in the early stages of conflict, and
would be protected only from the Azores to the
southwest approaches. This might ease the load on
surface combatants but lengthens the trans-Atlantic
voyage and could scarcely be more awkward for
supporting shore-based aircraft, unless ample use
could be made of airfields in France, Spain,
Portugal and the Azores as well as south-west
England.

In fact, wherever one looks there are problems of
scale and resources. It is clearly these, as well as the
change in the tactical situation discussed in Chapter
3, that have made many people, naval officers
included, doubt the continuing efficacy of convoy as
a means of ensuring the safe and timely arrival of
merchant shipping and the defeat of submarines
attempting to inhibit it. Their contention is that the
'Protected Lane' concept, by making the best use of
passive sonar with its much longer ranges, is more
economical in resources for similar trade-offs
between merchant ships and submarines sunk.

While seeing the force of the theory I have grave
misgivings about it, as I do also about the idea of
monster convoys of 300 ships or more. Both, in their
different ways, are invitations for the wolves to get
among the sheep. A protected lane would probably
be at least 50 miles wide, the front of a monster
convoy at anti-nuclear spacing at least 20. In the
noisy middle of either, the chances of detecting a
well-handled submarine from a vessel on the
periphery would not be high. A nuclear, in
particular, could make every torpedo tell and then
slip out of the back. Even if detected at that point it
might have to be left by escorts that had to keep up
with the convoy, or by lane protection units that
were more concerned with approaching threats.

My solution would be different and, while making
use of convoy and close escort, would bear more

Russians felt their northern bastion to be
reasonably secure. NATO units available in the
area were officially said in 1981 to number over 90
ASW surface ships, 70 submarines and 400 aircraft;
but these were by no means all for shipping
protection. For instance, the Royal Navy had to find
from those numbers its anti-submarine support for
the Atlantic Striking Fleet; many of the submarines
belonging to the smaller NATO navies were coastal
units; and most of the aircraft were at airfields
remote from the likely scene of action and not all

Top:
Replenishment groups too need anti-submarine protection. *Crown Copyright*

Above:
A World War 2 convoy. How appropriate is this kind of formation to modern conditions?
HMS *Vernon archives*

relation to the support-group concepts that were successfully introduced in the last two years of World War 2. Reasonably compact convoys of say 40 ships would be escorted by no more than four surface escorts, or better an Arapaho and three. This would leave enough surface forces to form at least three support groups which, operating at a distance from the convoys, must include towed-array ships, heavy helicopters for datum investigation and pouncing, and wide-area command and control. Each support group would ideally have at least one nuclear submarine operating with it, and have at its disposal one, better two, long range maritime patrol aircraft.

Convoys would be routed in accordance with three principles: to impose the maximum confusion and risk of exposure on enemy submarines; to get

the maximum benefit from the support groups; and to arrive on time. They would therefore not all follow the same track but there would be some similarity in their routes: call that a protected-lane concept if you will, but it is not really; some for example could pass north of a support group, some south, and support group areas could shift too. Finally, the judicious routeing of independents, some fitted with acoustic deception equipment which can surely be devised, could serve further to confuse the enemy.

The problems of an opposing submarine faced with this situation are considerable. He must, first, try to sort out what is going on up top. His shore authority, using satellite and other intelligence, may be able to help, but they can only tell him what has happened, not what is going to happen, and time-lags may be long. His sonic information will be as confused as Western organisation can make it. If he believes himself to be in the grain of a convoy, he may consider himself lucky but will probably have to use periscope some time. If well off track, he will have to use speed to get to a firing position; a conventionally-powered boat may even have to snort. Detection opportunities for the support groups and their associated aircraft, using radar and passive sonar, will be numerous. If the Soviet submarines resorted to group tactics, those opportunities would increase still further.

The intention would be to kill as many submarines as possible before they reached attacking positions, using the resources of the support groups. The close convoy escorts' chief purpose would be to frustrate submarines that had achieved firing positions and counter-attack those that did fire. Ship escorts could not linger to prosecute submarines once they had fallen astern of the convoy; but helicopters could, probably long enough to complete a kill, since they are fast enough to catch up. This is just one of the tremendous advantages that a few organic helicopters could give to each convoy's defence.

The whole scheme can best be expressed in the words once used to describe to me the flight deck and hangar operations of an aircraft carrier: a Roller-Bearing, Self-Adjusting Shambles. So long as it can confuse the enemy without getting out of

Allied control it seems likely to offer the best prospect of maintaining traffic flow, keeping shipping losses at an acceptable level and imposing high attrition on opposing submarines. It would be greatly helped by the acquisition of a dozen or so Arapaho outfits and associated helicopters: on American figures, these might cost about the same as four Type 22 frigates. So far as the other assets required are concerned, one could never have enough. But particularly if French and Spanish units could be included, three respectable support groups could certainly be put together, as well as the bare minimum of escorts, given the 1981 figures quoted; Royal Navy frigate numbers would have to be kept well above the 50 mark.

Fig 13
Convoy support group concept.

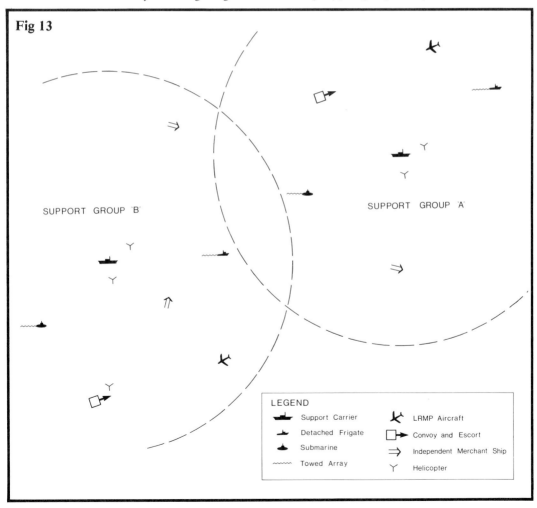

Fig 13

SUPPORT GROUP 'B'

SUPPORT GROUP 'A'

LEGEND

- ⬱ Support Carrier
- ⬱ Detached Frigate
- ⬱ Submarine
- ∿ Towed Array
- ⊀ LRMP Aircraft
- ☐▶ Convoy and Escort
- ⇒ Independent Merchant Ship
- Y Helicopter

Surface ASW assets in the Eastern Atlantic are very short by comparison with the task. Pictured here are HMS *Sirius,* (above) HMS *Broadsword* (right) and HNethMS *Tromp* (below) . Frigates like the Canadian HMCS *Skeena* (bottom) will have similar problems in the Western Atlantic.
Crown Copyright ; Rolls-Royce Limited

Inshore and Out of Area

Anti-submarine warfare ends only where the threat ends. The Soviet Union may not have many submarines to spare to conduct operations in the North Sea or the chops of the Channel, nor on the Southern Atlantic trade routes or in the Indian Ocean; but a few boats on either task could tie up a significant amount of Western forces.

The inshore problem is marginally the easier of the two because the resources can more readily be improvised from what is at hand. Fishery protection vessels, search and rescue helicopters and cross-channel ferries are not anti-submarine units, but all can be pressed into service in what is as much an operation of organisation and administration as it is of making war on the enemy. Naturally some specialised anti-submarine platforms will have to be made available, and others adapted; our own minefields put down to frustrate opposing submarines; and surveillance established. The main objectives must be to keep vital ports secure and open, and to ensure the passage of military supplies to Europe.

The out-of-area problem will need to be looked at in a coldly statistical light. If two Soviet submarines are at large in the Indian Ocean, they may sink 20 loaded tankers. Would that threat justify escorted convoys, with the inevitable depletion of resources elsewhere? Infinite variations will be possible on those figures, and it is quite possible that in those vast ocean spaces even convoys with a token escort or no escort at all would be a statistical best bet for many circumstances. There are resources in the areas, of course, but the United States Navy is unlikely to spare any for shipping protection, the French are mostly colonial administrative units and aircraft, and the British are likely to be hurrying back to the Eastern Atlantic. It is not a satisfactory situation, and in a war of long duration it would have to be rectified by the provision of forces from NATO nations, perhaps aided by contributions from Australia and Japan whose interest in the oil trade is as great as NATO's.

Barrier Operations

Barrier operations are different in kind from the others so far described. They are related entirely to the destruction of submarines and not to what NATO forces are trying to use the sea for. They are, in the jargon, sea-denial and not sea-use operations. But the attrition that they achieve on Soviet submarines, and the influence they have on the conduct of Soviet submarine operations, will naturally be of great value to NATO's sea use in general.

It is possible to envisage several barriers at or round geographical choke points such as the Bear Island/North Cape gap, the Gibraltar Strait, the Malta Narrows and the entrance to the Aegean Sea.

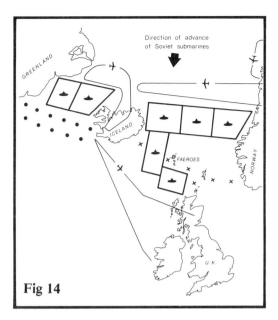

Fig 14

Fig 14
NATO ASW barrier: a Soviet view. This plan is adapted from one published in the Soviet press. Crosses represent the SOSUS arrays and the shading an anti-submarine minefield.

Below:
Realistic training can ensure the best use of resources. *Crown Copyright*

Fig 15
Building up to barrier operations: air patrols in peace and tension.

Each would need special treatment for its geographical and operational conditions. But the choke point and barrier that has received most publicity is that between Greenland, Iceland, the Faeroes and the United Kingdom.

The sea passages beween these pieces of land are rather more than 600 miles wide in total. The assets available to the West are bottom arrays, submarines both nuclear and conventionally powered, long range maritime patrol aircraft operating from bases conveniently close, and mines. Both Soviet and Allied sources have given some indication of possible barrier patterns; a Soviet view is shown on page 105, and some published illustrative NATO air patrol diagrams appear opposite. In summary, a resource bill of four or five long range maritime patrol aircraft airborne (meaning about 30 operational), six to eight submarines on station and a thousand CAPTOR mines is probably not too far out, for forces actually 'working the barrier'. You cannot thicken up more than that without unacceptably increasing the risk of mutual interference.

It is no wonder that the Soviet Union has shown a great deal of interest in, and apprehension of, an anti-submarine barrier here. Determined efforts can be expected in the direction of neutralising airfields in Iceland and Scotland, putting bottom arrays out of action by cutting sea cables or sabotaging shore terminals, minimising detection opportunities by careful programming of submarine transits, submarines 'bursting through' in groups and even perhaps incursions by surface forces.

Thus, in addition to the command, control and (most important of all) communication skills involved in setting up the barrier in the first place, there must be great inbuilt flexibility and adaptability to cope with enemy reactions and changes of tactic. Aircraft may have to lay and work sonobuoy fields much more frequently than expected if SOSUS is neutralised. Submarines may have to communicate with the outside world more often than they would like, if they are not getting results. Less or more reliance will have to be placed on CAPTOR in the light of early results. The barrier must not be over-dependent on a single component.

Nor must the whole of Allied strategy be over-dependent on the barrier. It would be silly not to exploit to the full the advantage the geography has given us. There is no way round the gaps for Soviet submarines coming from the north. But there are ways through, and Nitze's under-30% attrition rate is probably a fair estimate of the results to be expected even if pre-deployment of Soviet

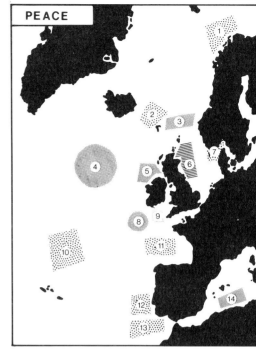

(a) PEACE

1. **Norwegian P-3 from Andoya – surface/sub-surface surveillance.**
2. **USN P-3 from Keflavik – surface surveillance.**
3. **Kinloss Nimrod – surface/subsurface surveillance**
4. **Kinloss Nimrod – surface surveillance of Soviet oceanographic research vessel.**
5. **St Mawgan Nimrod – trailing/updating Malin Head AGI.**
6. **Kinloss Nimrod – Tapestry**
7. **German Atlantic – surface surveillance.**
8. **Netherlands Atlantic operating from St Mawgan – Casex with UK submarine.**
9. **Vulcan – MRR training.**
10. **USN P3 from Lajes – surface surveillance of Soviet AGI bound for US Eastern seaboard.**
11. **French Atlantic – training with French task group.**
12. **Portugese C-130 – surface surveillance.**
13. **USN P3 from Rota – surface/subsurface surveillance.**
14. **Gibraltar based Nimrod – checking anchorages used by Soviet Mediterranean Squadron.**

Fig 15

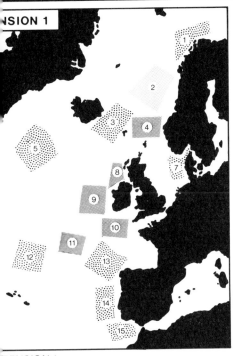

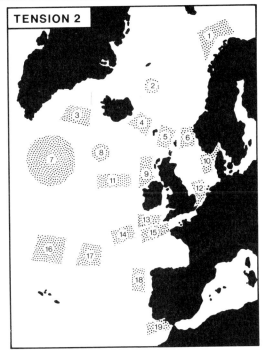

TENSION 1

1. Norwegian P3 from Andoya-surface subsurface surveillance.
2. Vulcan – MRR.
3. USN P-3 from Keflavik – surface/subsurface surveillance.
4. Kinloss Nimrod – subsurface surveillance.
5. USN P-3 from Keflavik-subsurface surveillance.
6. Not shown
7. German Atlantic – surface/subsurface surveillance
8. Kinloss Nimrod – subsurface surveillance.
9. St Mawgan Nimrod – surface surveillance.
10. Netherland Neptune operating from St Mawgan – surface surveillance.
11. St Mawgan Nimrod – surface/subsurface surveillance (SLOCS).
12. USN P3 from Lajes – surface/subsurface surveillance (SLOCS).
13. French Atlantic – surface surveillance.
14. Portugese C-130 –surface surveillance.
15. USN P-3 from Rota-surface/subsurface surveillance.

(c) TENSION 2

1. AIREASTLANT (Norwegian) P-3 – surface/subsurface surveillance.
2. AIREASTLANT (US) P-3 – shadowing Soviet surface attack group (SAG)
3. AIREASTLANT (US) P-3 – subsurface surveillance.
4. AIREASTLANT (US) P-3 – subsurface surveillance.
5. AIREASTLANT Nimrod – subsurface surveillance.
6. AIREASTLANT Nimrod – subsurface surveillance.
7. AIREASTLANT (US) P-3 – direct support to US Striking Fleet.
8. AIREASTLANT (Netherlands) Atlantic – shadowing Soviet SAG.
9. AIREASTLANT Nimrod – subsurface surveillance
10. GERNORSEA (German) Atlantic – surface/surface surveillance.
11. AIREASTLANT (US) P-3 – subsurface surveillance.
12. AIRCHAN (Netherlands) Neptune – surface surveillance.
13. AIREASTLANT Nimrod – subsurface surveillance (SLOCS).
14. AIREASTLANT Nimrod – subsurface surveillance (SLOCS).
15. AIREASTLANT Nimrod – subsurface surveillance (SLOCS).
16. WESTLANT (US) P-3 – surface surveillance (SLOCS).
17. WESTLANT (US— P-3 – subsurface surveillance (SLOCS)
18. IBERLANT (US) P-3 – surface surveillance.
19. IBERLANT (US) P-3 – subsurface surveillance.

submarines is not taken into account. So it would be even sillier to rely on the barrier to the detriment of other anti-submarine measures.

Contest in Depth

So I come to an unremarkable conclusion. Against a dangerous, numerous and technically improving enemy, bent on denying to NATO that use of the sea without which it cannot successfully conclude any war, the anti-submarine battle must be conceived as a contest in depth. The opponent must be faced with challenges at every moment of his deployment: to his intelligence, by facing him with the most confusing sonic picture that can be devised; to his security, by surveillance and the maximum spread of options for attacking him; to his offensive spirit, by ensuring that there are no easy targets to be had and by making sure he has to expose himself in order to get at any target. Given this philosophy, and plans and assets to match it, NATO can face the anti-submarine battle with some confidence.

Into the 1990s

Introduction

Since the first edition of this book was published in 1984, inevitably there have been changes in the pattern of anti-submarine warfare and the demands made of its practitioners. The direction of those changes was predictable, and in many cases was foreshadowed in the main text. Less predictable was the pace of change, which in general has been faster and more far-reaching than most people expected.

Strategically, the intervening years have seen the enunciation by the United States — with some acquiescence or endorsement by the rest of the NATO alliance — of a Maritime Strategy that owes much to assumptions about anti-submarine warfare and the correlation of forces in that field. This alone justifies a further look at the whole question.

Technically, advances have been made in the quality both of submarines and of the forces and systems that oppose them. But the advances have not been uniform; aided by research effort, by different positions on the learning curve — and in at least one case by a major espionage coup — some systems have been advanced technically to a far greater extent than their counters. There is a new balance, and it needs to be assessed. This new chapter follows the pattern of the previous ones, whose principles and basic facts are still valid.

The Threat

Strategic Background

In 1983, the Soviet Union was about to emerge from the Brezhnev period. This, after a decade of relative foreign-policy success for the Soviet Union, had degenerated from 1978 onwards towards stagnation and inertia. Some foreign adventures were beginning to look unprofitable, and the home economy was in a mess. The initiatives of President Gorbachev since his accession to power — according to most commentators — have been founded in a pragmatic attempt to solve these problems rather than any fundamental reappraisal of Marxist principles.

Thus, in spite of the newly fluid diplomatic and strategic scene — the effects of which may eventually be quite profound — we cannot look for any change in the Soviet Union's basic dynamism or its determination to guard the centre of Communist power. They will, as they have frequently told us, do what they think is necessary to preserve that integrity, and will make economic sacrifices in order to do so. According to most Western information sources, no slackening can be detected in the production rate of major Soviet arms systems. All that can be said — and this is held by certain analysts but by no means all — is that plans for further expansion may have been curtailed.

By contrast, the mid-1980s have seen some resurgence of morale in the West and particularly in the United States. This has allowed the emergence of more confident and forward policies, and nowhere more so than in the field of Maritime Strategy. This in the USA is now invariably spelt with a large M and S because of its articulation and extensive publicising in early 1986 by the then Secretary of the Navy and the Chief of Naval Operations.

The Maritime Strategy is declared to be based on the principle of deterrence, but makes great use of another element of alliance strategy — forward defence. Its avowed aim is to 'dilute (Soviet) effort, divert their attention, and force them to divide their forces'. Consequently it places great stress on putting the Soviet 'bastions' under pressure, and to this end to introducing powerful forces as early as possible into the Norwegian Sea and, probably, the Sea of Japan. Soviet forces held under threat are specifically to include SSBNs.

In this way, it is argued, any Soviet effort to interrupt sea communication across the Atlantic in war will be minimised because they will be preoccupied nearer home. Additional benefits will be a much less uncertain capacity to reinforce Norway; visible support to the ground forces in Europe; the attainment of a favourable end-of-war bargaining position through the attrition of the

Soviet 'insurance' force of SSBN; and, above all perhaps, the seizure and maintenance of the maritime initiative.

We will analyse these claims later in the light of the anti-submarine scene overall, but for the time being must turn to the technical changes in the threat, for they will much affect the outcome.

Technical Developments

Two new classes of Soviet submarine have made their appearance in the last six years. The 'Delta-IV' SSBN is, as its name implies, a development from the extensive 'Delta' class and was almost certainly built as a cheaper complement to the massive 'Typhoon' which continues in relatively slow production. The 'Delta-IV' carries 16 SS-N-23 missiles with a range of 4,500nm, so is fully capable of operating from the 'Bastions', but its humpbacked shape is not well suited to surfacing to fire from an under-ice position.

The other new boat is the 'Akula', a large (7,500 ton) nuclear-powered torpedo and tactical-missile-armed submarine with a steel hull. This, along with the 'Mike' and 'Sierra' which were mentioned in the 1984 edition as just making their appearance, poses something of a problem for the analyst: why three new classes of biggish tactical submarines, particularly as the huge 'Oscar' SSGN is still in slow series production? The circumstances of the recent loss of a 'Mike' class submarine in northern waters support the theory that it was an experimental type; probably no more will be built. That leaves two classes to follow two classes — 'Victor' and 'Alfa' — whose production has now ceased. The main differences between 'Akula' and 'Sierra' seem to lie in hull and reactor design rather than operational requirement: these look to be versatile boats, with both anti-surface and anti-submarine roles.

Weaponry has shown few radical developments. There is more talk than there was of a submarine-mounted anti-aircraft weapon that could be fired from submerged against a persistent helicopter, but there is no hard evidence in the literature. More plausible is the existence of a very large, long-range torpedo which is a wake-seeker for use against surface forces. This could increase the 'danger envelope' for high value units against Soviet submarines; but given the existence of subsurface-to-surface tactical missiles in substantial numbers already, any change is unlikely to be critical in tactical terms.

As was noted in the first edition, hull strength is a marked characteristic of new construction Soviet submarines, and there is no sign of any slackening of effort there. Double hulls, either one inside the other or in one case reputedly side-by-side, give great robustness against attack. The use of titanium hulls in certain classes gives not only strength but great diving depth. Much attention now seems to be paid to minimising weak points at hull openings in the way of valves and hatches.

But the most startling development, extending across the whole new generation of Soviet submarines including the 'Oscar' and 'Typhoon', is their quietness, brought on by improved propeller design and care over auxiliary machinery. This is said to have owed much to the American Walker spy ring in the early 1980s, and to unauthorised transfer of technology from Norwegian and Japanese sources at about the same time. Wherever it came from (and usually these developments are from several sources, well backed by a powerful research impetus at home) it has undoubtedly resulted in a dramatic advance. One American authority puts it at a reduction of 25dB in radiated noise levels since the late 1970s: that means that the actual sound pressures are about 3% of their previous values, and the effective range of any given passive acoustic sensor could be expected to be slashed by roughly 95%.

This is really the most telling change in the threat, and it has very considerable implications for the emphasis of anti-submarine operations, tactics and even strategy as we shall see. Three further points need to be made here. First, quietening is not confined to Soviet boats; third-party navies, which might in some circumstances be a threat, are in some cases being re-equipped with quieter submarines. Second, commensurate quietening of Western boats is not happening because they were pretty quiet already and the law of diminishing returns is operating. Third, there still will be — certainly up to the mid-1990s and probably to the end of the century — quite a proportion of noisy boats in all threat navies, including the Soviet.

The Means

The first point to be made from up-to-date evidence on the means of detecting submarines is that sound is still king. That is to say, the non-acoustic measures described on pages 42 and 43 have still, according to the latest analyses, nowhere reached anything approaching operational systems. It may be rash to say that on a commonsense assessment, given the very low level of signal and the large ambient variations, none of them ever will; but I should be prepared to wager that none will claim to be a *primary* (as opposed to a very minor, and very expensive, supplementary) system before the end of the century.

If sound is still king, what sort of sound? Clearly, the 1980s were the decade of the passive,

Above right and right:
A Soviet attack submarine of the 'Sierra' class which has been in production since the early 1980s.
USNIPC

110

particularly on the Western side; not only were targets helpful noise emitters, but equipments and processing were making rapid advances, the self-noise of platforms was being satisfactorily reduced and the command and co-ordination of ASW assets were making considerable strides. In these circumstances the great advantages of passive sonar, its long range against noisy targets and the security conferred by not transmitting, ensured that active means were used sparingly, often only to obtain a fire control solution in the final stages of the anti-submarine process.

To say all that had now changed, and active sonar was now the primary means of detection — let alone classification, localisation and tracking — would be a gross over-simplification of the situation. There is still a great deal to be said, observing the inherent advantages of passive sonar, for staying passive whenever it is operationally feasible: and I would suggest that means when a low encounter rate is acceptable, or when the expected targets are the noisier element of the opponent's submarine force, or when one's own tactics have a reasonable expectation of imposing noisy operation on the enemy.

There may also be technical advances that allow many or most of one's ASW platforms to remain passive. It is theoretically possible to conduct semi-active sonar searches, where a single powerful active transmitter insonifies an area of ocean and echoes are received by a number of listening units, enabling classification and the later stages of the ASW process to be carried out. Naturally this entails the closest co-ordination of the forces involved, and probably a sophisticated shore processing facility as well as excellent real-time communication.

Another technique that has been discussed, albeit in guarded terms, in the open literature is the relatively stealthy active sonar. This would be a fundamentally low-frequency equipment but with a 'spread spectrum' of transmission that would not advertise itself to anything like the same extent as the classical active sonar. It is difficult to see, however, how it could be linked in the semi-active mode with other units.

At the sharp end of the ASW process, there has been very little change in weapon concepts in the last five years. The intelligent torpedo is still the weapon of choice, indeed in the West it has made ground at the expense of both the conventional depth charge and the nuclear depth bomb, and it seems possible that the same goes for the Soviet Union as well. This is due to increased confidence in the torpedo as a reliable weapon, and that will be further discussed in the following section.

How then can one sum up the means of ASW as we approach the 1990s? They are not fundamentally different from the ones that were discussed in

the body of this book in 1984; the ASW process remains the same. The need for a multiplicity of assets, and their integration into a well co-ordinated campaign, appears in the face of a quieter, more sophisticated, better-armed and probably better-trained threat to be greater than ever.

The Weapons
It is as difficult as ever to define, in the ASW field, the boundaries between platforms and sensors and weapons, and to link one to another in a way that is clear to the reader. However, the method used in Chapter 4 is as good as any, and for consistency will be followed here.

Surface Ships
Large surface ships continue to be a focus of anti-submarine warfare because of their command and control facilities, their stock of airborne ASW assets, and — not least — their status as high value targets for submarines. There have been few significant changes in the past five years. American and Soviet carriers, only partly ASW-orientated in mission and evolutionary in design, have come into service at a stately pace; in European navies the mission has been more pointedly ASW and the rate relatively faster, with the completion of the British 'Invincible' class and the entry of the Italian *Giuseppe Garibaldi* and Spanish *Principe de Asturias* into service.

There has been no significant follow-through of the 'Arapaho' idea. The British experiment with HMS *Reliant*, which was in any case a rather over-cooked 'Arapaho' because it was a more or less permanent conversion, appears to have been unsuccessful and the ship has been withdrawn from service, to be replaced by the full-conversion, non-container-based *Argus*. This is no doubt a useful ship in both peace and war, and is welcome in its adoption of less-than-goldplated standards in a 'garage' unit, but it is not 'Arapaho'.

Smaller surface ships have shown more radical changes in ASW equipment. Most evidently, the ability to deploy a towed array has become common. In the US Navy, this equipment is most often the AN/SQR 18, but larger vessels like the 'Ticonderoga', 'Kidd', 'Spruance' and 'Arleigh Burke' classes, are fitted with the AN/SQR 19. The main difference is believed to lie in the inboard processing equipment; the 'wet end' is substantially similar in both.

Other navies in the Western orbit have shown much, but diverse, progress in towed array

development. Britain has been most active in the field, having started operational trials in the late 1970s. Its 2031 series towed arrays are now being fitted quite widely in the later frigate classes, and competitive feasibility studies are in hand by several consortia for the follow-up 2057 system. France is the only other country to have a home-grown towed-array programme, and this is still involved in an uneasy marriage with the variable depth sonars commonly fitted in French ships. However, the DBSV-61 towed array now appears to be in series production. The Netherlands, Spain, Canada, Australia and Japan have all announced fitting programmes based on the

American systems, particularly at the wet end; processing equipment varies more widely.

Towed arrays certainly have much increased the passive detection capabilities of surface ships and had submarines remained noisy they might have made a revolutionary impact, in spite of the need for towed-array units to keep operating speeds slow and to be stationed far from noisy friendly units — neither of which limitations is popular with commanding officers. How, in the new more silent threat environment, the towed array's effect may be maximised will be discussed below. Here one may only add that the towed array's potential as a receiver for semi-active (sometimes called Bistatic)

Left:
This view of the Type 23 Frigate HMS *Norfolk* depicts one of the first warships to have towed array capability as a primary element of its Staff Requirement. *Yarrow*

sonar using a remote transmitter has yet to be fully explored.

Surface ship active sonars have made little perceptible progress over the past five years. Partly, this was due to the confidence with which passive means were being viewed 10 to 15 years ago, when active-sonar research and development tended to take a back seat, and partly to conventional active sonars being far up the learning curve anyway. Improvements in hand are therefore incremental, as in the American SQS-53C and the British 2050, both developments of already operational sets. Driven by the new acoustic balance, active-sonar research may soon be boosted; if so, it is likely to be in the direction of remote transmitters (already mentioned), bottom-bounce (which requires great transmitted power and very large transducers) and spread spectrum (which while still needing power is not so self-advertising) or a combination of these techniques. Almost certainly, the vessels carrying transmitters for such advanced active sonars will need to have unusual underwater characteristics; small waterplane area twin hull (SWATH) ships are prime contenders. They will not be small — or at all cheap.

ASW weaponry specific to surface ships has undergone almost no development in the half-decade and the lightweight torpedo, covered in later paragraphs, remains the weapon of choice for ship-fitting.

Rotary Wing Aircraft

The new generation of medium-sized helicopters for operation from Frigates or destroyers has demonstrated its versatility. 'Everyone wants to use this bird', for above-water surveillance, over-the-horizon missile indication and control, utility tasks. In consequence its dedication to the ASW mission, whether search, screen or attack — which ideally requires 24hr readiness for the mission — is said to be in jeopardy. It is ironic that the helicopter associated with LAMPS-III, which was criticised for being conceived simply as an ASW offshoot of its parent ship, has become autonomous to this extent; the Lynx was of course always regarded as multi-role. In war, probably, the ASW mission would reassert itself, but good performance in war depends on adequate training in peace and it is to be hoped this is given proper priority.

Larger helicopters such as the SH-60 and Sea King continue on their sedate way. But it is interesting that one American commentator has

described the active-sonar dunker as 'the star of the show' in battle-group ASW; low on false alarm rates, high on reliability and regarded as a serious menace by opposing submarines. Plans for replacement of Western forces, with the SH-60F in the US Navy and the EH-101 in certain European navies, are well advanced; it is just as well, for such assets, particularly operating in the active mode, are likely to be critical in the new sonic situation wherever surface forces have to be protected. It is worth noting that many frigate-sized ships in the medium-power navies of the West are being designed to take the EH-101.

Tilt Rotor
Looking rather further ahead, the US Navy appeared to be pinning many hopes on the V-22 Osprey tilt-rotor aircraft in an ASW version. This has impressive dash and lift capabilities and might be expected to double the role of screen-and-pounce dunker with that of maritime patrol. But it is very large even for big-carrier operation and not many could be carried. As this chapter is written, the word is that no funding will be allowed for naval applications of this aircraft. But, in the USA, such projects have a habit of resurfacing and the story may not be ended. We must await events.

Fixed-Wing, Carrier-Based
With the V-22 halted, it is little wonder that some US Navy activists are advocating reopening the S-3 production line. This aircraft has indeed proved a very useful force multiplier in the 70s and 80s. However, confronted with a more silent and more often submerged enemy, and relying on radar and sonobuoys as sensors, it can expect sharply decreased detection rates in the future. Some people will, of course, cry 'then give us more aircraft'; but one wonders whether even the most affluent of societies can sustain that.

Fixed-Wing, Shore-Based
The Atlantique 2 and Nimrod 2 are now well into service and are by all accounts performing to their high specifications. The same goes for succeeding updates of the P-3 Orion; and a new generation of US Navy aircraft of this genre, based on the Boeing 757 airframe, is in prospect. But, given the dramatic quietening of the more modern Soviet submarines, the level of investment in this particular ASW system begins to come under question.

It is not that the aircraft have suddenly become useless. There will still be quite a few noisy targets for years to come, and against them the aircraft

may even be able to fulfil the dream of the mighty
lone hunter. They will certainly be important
assets in co-operation with other forces. In other
cases basically silent submarines may make
mistakes and expose themselves. In yet others, and
this will be explored further below, the tactics of
other ASW forces may be designed to give
maritime patrol aircraft detection opportunities.
But at the end of the day, passive means — which
have to be the basic sensors of these aircraft — are
going to have a low detection rate against quiet
submarines. Over-reliance on, or over-supply of,
maritime patrol aircraft is therefore to be guarded
against; cost-effectiveness must be the criterion.

Shipborne and Airborne Weapons

It is convenient to deal with shipborne and
airborne weapons together because, setting aside
the increasingly dated long-range ship-launched
nuclear systems, they are basically the same: depth
charges, which have not undergone significant
development lately, and lightweight torpedoes,
which have. Both the USA and Britain have
brought new systems into service. The American

torpedo is the Mk 50, faster, deeper-diving and
more discriminating than its predecessor the
Mk 46. To achieve its better physical performance
it uses a closed-cycle thermal engine of novel
design. The British Stingray, brought hurriedly
into service during the Falklands conflict, is more
conventionally powered with a seawater battery
and its speed and range performance is correspondingly less, but it has excellent diving depth
and is reputedly as clever as any in its
passive-active homing. Both these torpedoes have
'directed energy' warheads, which are said to
channel the available explosive force in the
optimum direction. Since the warheads are only 45
and 35kg respectively, they would certainly need
to be used to maximum effect against tough-
skinned, double-hulled Soviet submarines.

Submarines

If anything, there has been increased emphasis on
submarines as anti-submarine vehicles in the last
five years. The main impetus for this has been the
forward Maritime Strategy of the USA; there
were, clearly, areas where such a strategy could
best be implemented by submarines and one —
under the ice — where it could only be
implemented by submarines.

In order to carry out ASW missions, submarines
have been increasingly fitted with towed arrays.
American boats have the BQR-15 equipment, first
fitted in SSBNs for self-defence, and its develop-

ments; the British had initially a carbon-copy of this set in the 2023 and 2024 but have since proceeded along their own development track with the 2026 and, in new construction, 2046. Some of these arrays are of the 'clip-on' type, some are disposable. The French appear to be developing their surface-ship equipments for use by submarines.

But towed arrays are passive, and given the much quieter threat, attention is turning again to submarine-mounted active sonar. It is said that the size of some submarine designs now on the drawing board — notably the US SSN-21 'Seawolf' — is dictated by the need to mount a massive conformal array for the active mode. If this is so, it may very well be a spread-spectrum equipment, to minimise self-advertisement when transmitting.

Submarine ASW weaponry concentrates increasingly on the heavy, clever torpedo. The US Mk 48 Mod 5 ADCAP (Advanced Capability) is coming into service and is claimed to have better counter-measures (or maybe counter-counter-measures) and longer range. The British Spearfish, said to outdo the Mk 48 in range, speed and diving depth as well as guidance, should be in general service soon. All heavy torpedoes have the great advantage of carrying a large explosive charge, seven or eight times the weight of their airborne counterparts. This had led some commentators to suggest that there is no longer any need for nuclear anti-submarine weapons, and indeed the US Navy has announced that it is discarding nuclear SUBROC and ASROC heads. Moreover the replacement for SUBROC will not have a nuclear version. Whether that is entirely wise is open to question; it may be an advantage to have some nuclear charges available in case things get desperate. But there are still nuclear depth bombs, and it seems unlikely that the West would relinquish all its nuclear ASW weapons without a very substantial arms-control trade off.

Soviet ASW Systems

Most information about modern Soviet ASW systems is speculative, certainly in the open press. They are generally acknowledged to have applied more resources than the West on non-acoustic systems; equally generally, they are thought not to have got anywhere near deployment of an operational system in this field. So far as sonic systems are concerned, they have exploited towed array technology for submarines but it seems unlikely that their equipments are as advanced, or advancing as fast, as those in Western navies. Active sonars probably show less inferiority: it appears the Soviets use them more freely than Western counterparts, but this may be a measure of their shortcomings in the passive mode, or more emphasis on safety. They almost certainly lead the West in underwater communications and co-ordination of submerged submarines. Airborne ASW still seems to take a back seat, both in rotary and fixed-wing vehicles; however, it may be effective around the bases, and could not be ignored in the approaches to the bastions. Finally, information on modern Soviet anti-submarine weaponry remains exceptionally sketchy. They are presumed to have wire-guided heavy torpedoes with terminal homing for use from submarines. Ship-mounted systems are as described in Chapter 4: in summary, weapons covering a variety of ranges and delivering nuclear, conventional depth-charge or homing-torpedo warheads. It is also assumed that air-dropped ASW torpedoes can be deployed.

The Anti-Submarine Battle
Background
The USA's Maritime Strategy, remarked upon at the start of this Chapter, must have a profound effect on any analysis of how the ASW battle might go in the 1990s. Forward operations are now openly stated to be the means of preoccupying the Soviet Navy, and particularly its submarine force, so that it cannot concentrate on the 'sea lines of communication' that are vital to NATO in a major conflict. By contrast, it appears that the direct defence of shipping — convoy, escort and support — is to be de-emphasised; some interpretations of the Strategy suggest it would be virtually discarded.

It must be remembered that ASW is only half the battle, particularly in areas where Soviet air power can be brought to bear, as it assuredly can in the northern Norwegian Sea. Some analysis of that factor may be found in my *Air Defence at Sea* (Ian Allan, 1988) and it is worth quoting here one remark I made in it which can be applied to both undersea and above-water warfare: 'The Strategy . . . is by no means risk-free. It embodies two concepts which historically have been the prerogative of the stronger naval power: blockade of the enemy fleet, and seeking a decisive battle . . . The United States Navy . . . would have to cope with submarines; and, even more, would have to absorb the severe air threat . . . very strong forces will be needed.'

My conclusion was far from clear-cut, even in the air defence field: 'if anyone can do it, the USN can'. How are they likely to fare on the ASW side; and will it have the desired effect of relieving pressure on shipping crossing the Atlantic?

Threatening the Soviet Strategic Submarine Force
All the indications are that the Soviet SSBN force will largely be stationed in waters relatively close to home, will make increasing use of under-the-ice operations and will be supported by a proportion of the modern SSNs. More and more of the submarines will be intrinsically quiet and SSBNs operate quietly by habit.

Sending SSNs to go hunting for such submarines in the vast spaces of the Arctic Ocean does look to be a business of very little return for (potentially) enormous effort. To read the work of some American writers, you would think it was simply a matter of going around picking off the clanking old things as they lurked. It is not going to be like that in the 1990s. The encounter rate is likely to be very low indeed, in spite of towed arrays, in spite of increased Western expertise in under-ice operation.

That is not to say the option ought to be discarded altogether. Soviet sensitivity to the security of their SSBN force is well known, and to

Below:
Under-ice operations are now being emphasised in Western SSN training. Here two British submarines rendezvous at the North Pole with two RAF Nimrods. *Crown Copyright*

Inset:
P-3 Orion updates continue: the airframe may be old and dull but it works, and it is what is inside that counts. *RAAF*

An RAF Nimrod stands by to receive its load of sonobuoys. *Dowty*

play on it is a legitimate Western strategic device. They must be made to feel that if they denude their SSBN forces of protection, they take a risk. Therefore, the art must be kept alive and forces expert; how many of them are used in this role, if the Strategy has to be put into effect, will be for the commander of the day to decide.

Control in Vital Sea Areas

While there may be several areas in a NATO/Warsaw Pact conflict that may be regarded as vital for sea use, it is sufficient to take the Norwegian Sea case as was done in Chapter 5.

US commentators on the Maritime Strategy are increasingly likely to say the Strategy does not necessarily mean that the Strike Fleet will advance like an army with banners into the Norwegian Sea at the first sign of tension. Some imply that they will not go there until sufficient attrition has been imposed on the Soviet submarine force. That may be a wise policy, but how is the attrition to be wrought without some focus, some bait for the Soviet submarines? Mere hunting will not do it against quiet submarines, that is for sure.

It looks as though the brunt might be borne by the European forces in the area, notably any amphibious forces reinforcing north Norway, the British ASW carrier group probably escorting such forces, the NATO Standing Naval Force Atlantic, other north European NATO units, shore-based maritime patrol aircraft, and any diversionary or deception units put into the area. These last might have a key role: not only would they attract submarines that might otherwise attack high value targets, they could by confusing the underwater sound-picture induce basically quiet submarines to act indiscreetly. It is the same technique as was suggested for shipping protection in Chapter 5, but even more studied and structured.

That sort of thing would surely be needed. For a failure to bring Soviet submarines to action in the early stages of such a scenario could have two quite nasty effects. First, a proportion of the submarines could creep through on to the shipping routes in the Atlantic. Second, the rest could still be lying in wait for the Strike Fleet when it did arrive; and in a desperate European war, the pressures on it to go in as early as possible would be great. It would, at the very least, arrive in what was still a hostile submarine environment.

If anything, the complexities of water space management and co-ordination would then seem to have increased as the 1990s are approached. Passive detections and classifications will be less frequent and less certain, false alarms probably more frequent, the need for deep processing and analysis of all the available data more urgent than ever. It is here that there may be a good deal of hope: the intrinsic capacity of processing systems, particularly shore-based ones, has vastly increased lately and 'cueing' of ASW units on to indications of submarine activity is put forward as a real gain. One hopes that is so; it depends on good communications to and from forces at sea, putting a premium on those that can so communicate.

Protection of Shipping

It will be clear from the above analysis that I do not subscribe to the view that the Maritime Strategy means shipping can be left to itself. History suggests that this would be folly; the appalling story of US shipping losses off the east coast of the USA in 1942, and the Japanese failure to protect shipping in the Pacific throughout World War 2 tell their own story. There is absolutely nothing to suggest that if the Soviet Union decided on a submarine campaign against transatlantic shipping, the Maritime Strategy would do more than dilute it somewhat. That judgement is hardened by the advances in Soviet submarine quietening, which means that transitters would have a much better chance of slipping through the air and submarine barriers which depend so critically on passive sonar.

Nor do I consider that the basic philosophy of convoy defence and support groups, put forward in Chapter 5, is invalidated by subsequent develop-ments. There may, however, be a need for more emphasis on active sonar in convoy escorts, and here the best (and most quickly achieved) force multiplier is undoubtedly the helicopter. Again,

one hopes the Arapaho idea is not being allowed to die, particularly in the USA, where they ought to be able to afford some development (it would only be a tiny fraction of the amount that could be spent on the Strategic Defence Initiative).

Other Seas, Other Battles

There are now over 40 states with submarine forces, mostly small in numbers and of variable efficiency but generally with modern, small, handy submarines. These are often impressively quiet but their endurance is limited. Much has been made of the possibility of increased underwater perfor-mance given by new advanced propulsion systems: this may come in the late 1990s. The larger, wider-ranging navies must take increased account of such threats: after all, conflict is much more likely against or between the owners of these small navies than it is between the superpowers or their blocs.

In general, the principles of ASW continue to apply under such conditions. The idea of the protected force is likely to be more effective than that of the unalerted hunt; the imposition of unfavourable tactical conditions on the opposition, by manoeuvre, by disposition, by deception, and the co-ordination of both information and of operations, are likely to be just as critical. The main lesson of the Falklands, that a high state of training and professionalism is the biggest force multiplier of all, must never be lost.

Summary

A recent book by Richard Compton-Hall, *Submarine versus Submarine*, gave the most significant indication yet seen of the way in which anti-submarine warfare is changing. He generates, from a deliberately sketchy politico-military scenario, a series of incidents to illustrate his theme. It is notable that in every incident but one he has had to invent a set of coincidences — indiscreet operation, material failure, faulty maintenance, communication difficulty — which alert the participants and lead to an encounter. As a submariner of great experience, he is quick to point out that such things happen. But, in time of extreme tension or war, would they happen often enough to make a forward strategy work?

We have seen that the forward strategy has two purposes: to impose attrition on Soviet submarines and to preoccupy them in tasks far from the 'sea lines of communication'. In the environment of the 1990s it is doubtful if the first purpose can be effectively implemented by forward operations. Partly because of that, it is by no means certain that the Soviet Navy would co-operate on the second. Nor, if it chose to conduct an oceanic anti-shipping campaign, would its more modern submarines have so much difficulty negotiating the barriers as their forerunners. However great the acoustic gain of towed arrays, modern sonobuoys and submarine passive sonars, it does not on all the evidence appear to have kept pace with the quietening of the new generation of Soviet submarines.

Therefore the direct defence and indirect support of organised surface shipping, both combatant forces and merchant ships, appears to me to be gaining and not lessening in importance as we approach the 1990s. It is an art that was in danger of becoming neglected in the decade that we are leaving, and it must be to some extent relearnt in modern conditions. By tactical disposition and movement, and by liberal use of deception measures both acoustic and above-water, opposing submarines must be made to expose themselves if they want to get into an attacking position. If the do not choose to do so, well and good. Donald Macintyre, arguably the greatest anti-submarine practitioner of World War 2, took as much pride in losing only two ships from convoy in two years (1941-43) as he did in sinking two U-boats during that time.

Not only the employment but the shape of anti-submarine forces will need to be modified to meet the new conditions. This cannot be done quickly and it will in any case be a matter of changed emphasis, not revolution. Passive systems will have to concentrate on high-gain devices and those will tend to be large and expensive: thinline towed arrays, sensitive sonobuoys. With greater stress on directed use, the necessary economy may be achieved. If there is to be proliferation, it should now be in active systems, particularly helicopters with dipping sonars. The necessary decks and embarked maintenance facilities should be made available, not all of them necessarily in active fleet units. For the longer term, semi-active sonars should be given higher priority for research and development.

Dramatic turning points are not usual in maritime affairs in peacetime, and when they do happen tend not to be apparent at the time. But it does seem that in ASW the turn of the 1990s will see such a twist in the road. That it leads back into more classical ways of approaching the problem does not surprise the experienced; but it is likely to be deeply unpalatable to the US Navy. As is often the way in that great country, they have been borne forward on a wave of confidence. The offensive spirit is deeply ingrained. That is a military virtue, but it must not be naïvely employed; the stakes are too high. If their friends think they have got it wrong, then it is only friendly that they should tell them so.

Below:
The Dowty advanced 99-channel sonobuoy receiver selected for the EH-101 programme. *Dowty*

Epilogue

The Basilisk's Tale

In the forenoon of 4 October 1937 HMS *Basilisk*, with *Boreas* in company, was on patrol in the Western Mediterranean. The Nyon Arrangement, designed to halt 'piratical' depredations by submarines supporting General Franco in the Spanish Civil War, had been in force for a fortnight, and *Basilisk's* patrol was the sharp end of it. Asdic operators were closed up and everyone on the alert.

At a time which is not now clear from the records but looks to have been about 8.30am – soon after the change of watch – the Asdic cabinet reported an echo, and for the next quarter of an hour this was investigated using the standard procedures. Then the drama intensified. No less than eight of the *Basilisk's* company saw what appeared to be a torpedo track approaching from up-sun and passing down the starboard side. Depth charge crews were closed up and an attack delivered on the echo, now firmly classified as a submarine. Contact was lost after the attack but regained about an hour later, when a second attack was delivered. There was no contact thereafter, but neither were there any debris, oil or other sign of a submarine sinking.

The incident, swiftly reported, brought an equally swift reaction from the First Sea Lord, Lord Chatfield. The apparent escape of a submarine that had attacked a destroyer cast doubt on the efficiency of the Fleet's anti-submarine measures, on which so much confidence had been placed. What was to be done? The Commander-in-Chief, Mediterranean (Admiral Sir Dudley Pound in his heyday) agreed:

'If a submarine was depth-charged by *Basilisk* it ought to have been destroyed and if there was no submarine we cannot say so without acknowledging the unreliability of Asdics.'

He added that he was not convinced that a submarine was involved, and had instructed the Vice Admiral of the Battle Cruiser Squadron to conduct an enquiry.

The report of this enquiry, completed on 7 October, found that there was no submarine and no torpedo. Many inconsistencies were discovered in eye-witness accounts, tracks and sonic and attack data. Moreover *Boreas*, with a highly experienced operator, had had no confirmed Asdic contact. The episode was put down to the inexperience of *Basilisk's* anti-submarine team – the ship was newly out of refit – and the importance of training in Mediterranean conditions emphasised. Chatfield had the last word, as he usually did; at the end of an involved docket discussing rules of engagement and citing the *Basilisk* incident, he minuted:

'No action is required since the Basilisk incident did not take place'.

It was a good way to close a file, but there were lessons which may not have been taken enough to heart. Certainly the Fleet's confidence in Asdics was undiminished, and the pride with which they were demonstrated to Winston Churchill off Portland in 1938 was genuine. He wrote afterwards to Chatfield:

'What surprised me was the clarity and force of the (Asdic) indications. . . I never imagined that I should have heard one of these creatures asking to be destroyed. It is a marvellous system and achievement.'

Capt Basil Jones, who was in HMS *Walpole* with Churchill at the time, wrote later:

'. . . underwater acoustics were perfect. Smoke candles appeared at the stern from the submarines attacked with unnatural accuracy, but without cheating.'

That was a far cry from the tension, urgency and frustration in the *Basilisk* less than a year earlier. But there were harder lessons ahead, a great deal of fire and blood and drowning in icy seas. Of course they would not have been avoided entirely even by a comprehensive anti-submarine system making more use of aircraft, small handy escorts and electronic aids, all of which could have been developed much more vigorously before the war began; but the effect of the U-boat campaign would have been much mitigated and the crisis of 1942 and early 1943 would have been milder or would not have occurred at all.

The lessons endure. Reliance on a single system, or a limited-area combination of two or three systems, is foolhardy in anti-submarine warfare at any time. It is madness when those systems are untried in war.

Everything in my studies of anti-submarine warfare leads me to the conclusion that because it deals with an enemy possessing great power and many options, covers a number of diverse British and Allied objectives, occurs in a complex and imperfectly-understood medium and allows a great variety of technologies, it must be comprehensive in its scope and integrated in its conception and control.

The theoretical attractions of a forward strategy are considerable: playing on the known preoccupations of the opponent, carrying the fight to points where he is sensitive and away from areas where we are vulnerable. But it is dependent on the opponent's own view of the matter at the time, and that may be quite different from what one expected. It is also dependent on many unproven technical assumptions and some of these, as the past decade has shown, are subject to quite rapid change.

Five years ago, in the Epilogue to the First Edition of this book, I wrote: 'If we become obsessed with a single threat or scenario; if we rely too much on passive acoustic methods and forget that opponents may get quieter; if we put our trust in distant methods and forget that some submar-ines will always get through; if we think our peacetime efficiencies in detection and weapon effectiveness will hold good in wartime conditions: then we shall pay, if deterrence fails.'

Events in the meantime have reinforced all that. And it is a pity, given the acknowledged British expertise in this field of maritime warfare — which is something that must not be lost to the Alliance — that the Ministry of Defence has on the evidence of recent Parliamentary Papers given such total support to the thinly-based strategy of forward operations. It may satisfy the accountants and the operational analysts, but they are not the people who will have to see shipping through to the reinforcement terminals.

It is not even as though, given the lower noise levels of Soviet submarines, the forward deployment of a mainly passive-sensor outfit is an evidently economical solution. That it is increasingly shaky in operational terms is beyond doubt. That is not to say that money must be thrown at everything; though I would always argue that ASW assets should not be starved or neglected, I hope it has been shown in this book that there are ways of employing them to the best advantage, and a few devices both material and tactical that compound the problems of any submarine trying to get to grips.

Bibliography

There are no standard text-books on anti-submarine warfare in the open literature, and I claimed no access to classified sources. However, on the various aspects there is in fact a good deal of published work, and it is from these fragments that I have tried to build up the whole. The list below is not exhaustive, but gives the principal sources.

Chapter 1: Historical material is culled from the histories of HMS *Vernon*, HMS *Osprey* and the Anti-Submarine Division of the Admiralty, which as well as the Naval Staff Histories produced in 1942 a very informative account of the pioneering work in ASW from 1905 onwards. World War 2 source books included, notably, Capt S.W. Roskill's *The War at Sea* (HMSO, 1954) and Cdr Richard Compton-Hall's *The Underwater War 1939-45* (Blandford, 1982).

Chapter 2: The writing on Soviet objectives and naval philosophy comes mainly from V.D. Sokolovsky's *Military Strategy* and Admiral of the Fleet of the Soviet Union S.G. Gorshkov's *The Sea Power of the State* (Pergamon Press, 1978). Much reference was also made to books and papers by Professor Michael MccGwire of the Brookings Institute; James McConnell and Bradford Dismukes' *Soviet Naval Diplomacy* (Pergamon Press, 1979); Paul H. Nitze and others' *Securing the Seas: the Soviet Naval Challenge and Western Alliance Options* (Westview Press, 1979); James Cable's *Gunboat Diplomacy* and *Britain's Naval Future* (Macmillan, 1981 and 1983). Other useful sources were the October 1982 issue of the United States Naval Institute *Proceedings,* and articles by Milan Vego both there and in the *Journal* of the

Below:
A German frigate designed for North Sea anti-submarine work. The freeboard is low and since helicopters come from shore there is no helicopter deck or hangar. *NATO photograph*

Royal United Service Institute and the US War College *Review*. The Argentine account of the *San Luis* appeared in the *International Defense Review* of January 1983. Factual information on threat navies came from *Jane's Fighting Ships* and the International Institute for Strategic Studies' *The Military Balance*, 1982-83.

Chapter 3: For basic acoustic theory, the best sources were R.J. Urick's *Sound Propagation in the Sea* (DARPA, 1979) and Kosta Tsipis in *The Future of the Sea Based Deterrent* (MIT Press, 1973) and *Tactical and Strategic Anti-Submarine Warfare* (SIPRI/MIT Press, 1974). On the general principles and practice of ASW, Richard L. Garwin in *The Future of the Sea Based Deterrent*, Joel S. Wit's 'Advance in Anti-Submarine Warfare' *(Scientific American*, February 1981), Jim Bussert's 'Computers add new Effectiveness to SOSUS/, CAESAR' *(Defense Electronics*, October 1979) and Norman Friedman's 'Is the Nuclear Submarine Really Invulnerable?' *(Defence*, January/February 1982), were most valuable, and reference was also made to Roland J. Starkey Jr.'s series in *Military Electronics and Countermeasures* in 1981. On non-acoustic detection, extensive recourse was made to papers, some of them still unpublished, by Professor Michael MccGwire and Dr. Donald C. Daniel; both of them kindly gave permission for their use as background. When it came to putting the ASW process together, several further publications were of great value, including the North Atlantic Assembly's pamphlet *NATO Anti-Submarine Warfare: Strategy, Requirements and the Need for Co-Operation* (1982), Rear-Adm Martin Wemyss' 'Submarines and Anti-Submarine Operations for the Uninitiated' (RUSI *Journal*, September 1981), AM Sir John Curtiss' 'Destruction of Enemy Submarines from the Air' *(NATO's 15 Nations)* and AVM G.A. Chesworth's 'Maritime Alliance: Practice and Future' (RUSI *Maritime Strategy* Seminar, October 1981).

Chapter 4: The main sources for factual information were *Jane's Fighting Ships, Weapon Systems and all the World's Aircraft*. I cannot but accord priority to these fine works of reference. However a large number of other sources were consulted, including promotional literature from firms (Plessey Electronic Systems, Marconi Underwater Systems, Marconi Avionics, EH Industries, Bofors AB, Gould, Inc, and the General Electric Company); Wit and Bussert (see under Chapter 3); one particular issue of the *International Defense Review* (March, 1983) containing articles by Gowri S. Sundaram and Norman Friedman, as well as many other snippets in other issues of this excellent journal; articles by Lockheed representatives in *Navy International* and *Defense* (May and June 1979); and Lt-Cdr Stephen R. Arends' 'Management of ASW Systems' in the US Naval War College *Review* of March/April 1979, which although essentially a plea for the active-sonar helicopter gave a good run-down on many other systems.

Chapter 5: The standard NATO case is drawn from many sources but the two best expositions are probably in the works already cited, the North Atlantic Assembly pamphlet and the Nitze study. On this I have built my own views, and these are to some extent an expansion of ideas already put forward in *The Royal Navy Today and Tomorrow* (Ian Allan, 1981) and 'Submarine Attacks on Shipping' *(Naval Forces*, June 1982).

Chapter 6: Main sources for 'Into the 1990s' were the *Proceedings of the United States Naval Institute*; the periodical *Military Technology*; and the work of Donald C. Daniel, particularly *Anti-Submarine Warfare and Superpower Strategic Stability* (Mac-Millan, 1986).

Chapter 7: The *Basilisk's* tale is in file Adm. 116/3529 in the Public Record Office.